Jean Insinga

# Simply Accounting™

## PRACTICE SETS

PRENTICE HALL, Upper Saddle River, New Jersey 07458

Disk Included

Practice Sets and Manual by Jean S. Insinga, MS, CAIS.

Production manager: Richard Bretan
Acquisions editor: Diane de Castro
Executive editor: P.J. Boardman
Manufacturing buyer: Ken Clinton


Simon & Schuster / A Viacom Company
Upper Saddle River, New Jersey 07458



Printed in the United States of America
10 9 8

ISBN 0-13-348764-4

Prentice-Hall International (UK) Limited, *London*
Prentice-Hall of Australia Pty. Limited, *Sydney*
Prentice-Hall Canada Inc., *Toronto*
Prentice-Hall Hispanoamericana, S.A., *Mexico*
Prentice-Hall of India Private Limited, *New Delhi*
Prentice-Hall of Japan, Inc., *Tokyo*
Simon & Schuster Asia Pte. Ltd., *Singapore*
Editora Prentice-Hall do Brasil, Ltda., *Rio de Janeiro*

# CA-Simply Accounting Practice Sets

*Practice Sets and Manual by*
Jean S. Insinga

*PRENTICE HALL*
*Upper Saddle River, New Jersey 07458*

***Acknowledgments***

*Special thanks to Nancy L. Kelly, friend and colleague and Robert Gill, MXCTC Accounting and Information Systems graduate who both gave their time and expertise in reviewing and editing the practice sets.*

# TABLE OF CONTENTS

# Preface

The CA- Simply Accounting program practice sets are designed to provide the business student with the experience to convert a manual accounting system to a computerized accounting system. The experience gained will better prepare the student for the job market. The practice set book begins with the the necessary instructions to begin and work with CA-Simply Accounting for Windows, as well as a step by step guide using the General Ledger with a sample company.

The book contains three practice sets, with an increasing level of difficulty. The Greenthumb Landscaping Company is a sole proprietorship service company, using the General Ledger. Krystal's Boutique is a sales and service corporation, using the general ledger, accounts payable, and accounts receivable modules. Each practice set requires students to record transactions on journal entry forms for a one month period and to enter these transactions into the computer. The student is required to print the necessary financial statements, backup data files, and close the accounting period. Estimated time for each practice set is approximately 8 to 10 hours.

The Energy Connection is a sales and service corporation. The student will use the General Ledger, Accounts Payable, Accounts Receivable, Inventory Control, and Payroll modules. This practice set requires the student to analyze and enter transactions in the appropriate module, for the first three months of a fiscal year. The student will complete the accounting cycle for each month, entering adjusting entries, printing all financial statements, backing up data files for each module, and printing quarterly reports for payroll. Estimated completion time for the practice set is 18 to 20 hours.

The use of the practice sets will better develop a student's understanding of computerized accounting systems as used in a service and merchandising company. The purpose of computerizing a company's records is to create accurate and timely reports to improve business decisions. The success of a company depends on the economy and how well a company is managed. Computers are used as a tool in most businesses. The students will integrate their knowledge of accounting with the accounting software.

# Introduction

## Overview

The CA-Simply Accounting Windows Program is a real-world, real-time integrated accounting package, designed specifically for small businesses. The general ledger, accounts payable, accounts receivable, inventory control, and payroll modules work together in organizing a business's accounting records. CA-Simply Accounting is designed to help your business operate more accurately and efficiently.

CA-Simply Accounting is designed to meet the needs of first-year accounting students. The student will analyze and record the transactions on the forms provided and then record the entry in the general journal. The CA-Simply accounting will post the entries to the ledger and produce all the necessary financial reports.

## What This Package Contains

This package contains the program disk, the data disk (3.5 inch media) and the practice set book.

# Chapter 1

## Using CA-Simply Accounting

### Overview

CA-Simply Accounting for Windows is an integrated accounting software package consisting of General Ledger, Accounts Receivable, Accounts Payable, Inventory Control and Payroll Modules. In this chapter you will compare the manual and computerized accounting systems and learn basic computer operations to run CA-Simply Accounting for Windows.

### Objectives

After completing this chapter, you will be able to:

1. Compare the manual and computerized accounting system.
2. Install CA-Simply Accounting.
3. Access the CA-Simply Accounting Program.
4. Work with the practice company.
5. Backup data files.
6. Exiting CA-Simply.

### Preparing the System

**Hardware and Software Requirements**
The minimum software and hardware your computer system needs to run both Windows and Simply Accounting successfully are:

- CA-Simply Accounting for Microsoft Windows.
- MS-DOS or PC-DOS, version 3.1 or later.
- Microsoft Windows, version 3.1 or later.
- A computer that can run Microsoft Windows in enhanced mode.
- A hard disk drive and at least one floppy disk drive.

- A VGA or similar high resolution monitor that is supported by Windows.
- A printer that is supported by Windows, to print reports, statements, checks and invoices.
- A mouse that is supported by Windows.

## Installing the Program

### Make a backup copy

Before installing, use File Manager to make backup copies of your CA-Simply Accounting disks.
From the Program Manager:

- Click **Main Icon**.
- Click **File Manager**.
- Click **Disk** from the menu bar.
- Click **Copy Disk**.

Warning displays for destination disk.

- Click **OK**, if correct drive is designated.
- Place Disk One in the disk drive as the Source Disk and click **OK**.

You will be prompted for the Destination disk.

- Remove the Source Disk and place the blank destination disk in the drive.
- When the copy is complete, remove the disk and repeat the steps for the remaining disks.
- Exit the Program Manager.

**To install CA-Accounting on your computer's hard disk, follow these steps:**

- Insert the CA-Simply Accounting Program disk in your computer's floppy disk drive.
- From the Program Manager, click **File**.
- Click **Run**.
- Type **A:INSTALL** and press < **enter** >
- Click **OK** to accept the path displayed or enter new path.
- Click **Install** to install all files displayed.

The message Installation Complete will display. Click **OK**. Store the CA-Simply Account disks in a safe place after installation. Window 3.1 and 3.11 users will see an Simply Accounting Icon.

Window 95 users must create a shortcut to activate program from the start menu.

**To create a shortcut:**

- Click Start.
- Click **Settings**.
- Click **Taskbar.**
- Click **the Start Menu programs tab.**
- Click **Add**.
- Type file name or click Browse. After clicking Browse - Double Click the file Winsim.
- Click the Icon with right mouse button and drag a copy off the box.
- Escape from the box.

**Using the Mouse or Keyboard keys:**

| | |
|---|---|
| ***Click*** | Press the left mouse button once. |
| ***Double click*** | Press the left mouse button twice quickly. |
| ***Scroll*** | Click the scroll bars (bars with arrows left or right or up or down) moving the list up or down or left to right. |
| ***Select*** | Click the mouse or Press the ALT key and underlined letter of the menu item. |
| ***TAB key*** | Move between fields. |
| ***Shift + Tab Key*** | Move in the reverse direction. |

**Using the Window Work Area**

| | |
|---|---|
| ***Main Window*** | Main Window of CA-Simply Accounting. |
| ***Menu*** | List of choices. |
| ***Dialog Box*** | Window displaying various information boxes. |
| ***Scroll Bars*** | Move the window from left to right or up or down. |
| ***List Box*** | Drop down window to select from a list of choices. |
| ***Check Boxes*** | Click with an X to turn on or Click to remove the X to turn off. |
| ***Command Buttons*** | Click command buttons such as OK, Cancel, Distribute, Post, Browse or Define **OR**<br>Tab to the Button **OR**<br>Press ALT + the underlined letter of the button. |

| | |
|---|---|
| ***Close a Window*** | Double-click the Control menu box in the upper left corner of the window. (-) **OR**<br>Press ALT + Spacebar to open the Control menu, then press C to close **OR**<br>Press ALT + F4. |
| ***Get Help*** | Press F1 and select one of the choices from the Help menu **OR**<br>Click the F1= Help tool button **OR**<br>Drag the button for which you want help to the F1= Help tool button **OR**<br>Drag the F1= Help tool button to the button for which you want help. |
| ***Exit the Program*** | Double click the Control menu in the upper left corner of the main Window ( Opening Window) **OR**.<br>From the main Window, press ALT + Spacebar to open the Control menu, then press C to close **OR**<br>Press ALT + F4. |

You do not have to be a computer expert to use CA-Simply Accounting System, and you will find this double-entry accounting system powerful, yet the easiest to use of all packages now available for the IBM PC and compatible computers. However, you should have some basic knowledge about the computer operations. Before accessing the CA-Simply program, let's compare the manual accounting to computerized accounting steps.

## Comparing the Manual and the Computerized Accounting System

Notice the similarities between manual and computerized accounting. The accounting steps that you are learning from your textbook are the same. For example, in manual accounting, you use a worksheet to prepare a trial balance. With a computer program, the trial balance is prepared automatically for you when the journal entries are posted to the general ledger.

In addition, with a computer program, financial reports such as the income statement and balance sheet are automatically and continuously updated for you whenever entries are posted to the general ledger. In contrast, usually in manual accounting, these reports are updated only after you enter and compute adjusting entries because of the labor involved in manually re-computing the general ledger for each transaction.

As a result, with an integrated accounting program, you can immediately and easily have a real-time picture of the financial status of a company to project which areas to concentrate on, for example, sales, inventory management, or personnel overhead.

**Steps in the Accounting Cycle**

| Manual Steps: | Computerized Steps: |
|---|---|
| 1. Start with the account balances in the ledger at the beginning of the period. | 1. Create the chart of accounts, enter the beginning balances. |
| 2. Analyze and journalize transactions as they occur. | 2. Analyze transactions and enter them in the computer, which automatically prepares a journal that can be printed at any time. |
| 3. Post journal entries to the ledger accounts. | 3. The computer posts from the journal to the ledger. |
| 4. Compute the unadjusted balance in each account at the end of the period. | 4. The computer computes the balance in each account. You can view or print updated financial reports at any time. |
| 5. Enter the trial balance on the worksheet and complete the worksheet. | 5. The computer prepares a trial balance. Enter adjusting entries in the computer. No worksheet is needed. |
| 6. Using the worksheet as a guide:<br>a. Prepare the financial statements.<br>b. Journalize and post the adjusting entries.<br>c. Journalize and post closing entries. | 6. The computer prepares the financial statements and posts the adjusting and closing entries. |
| 7. Prepare the post-closing trial balance. | 7. The computer prepares the post-closing trial balance. |

## Accessing the CA-Simply Program

To begin a session using CA-Simply, you will need the data disk containing the practice sets used in this book. To become familiar with CA-Simply, the Practice Company data files will be used. You will be given a trial balance and a list of transactions to record in the journal. After completing the journalizing, you will print the trial balance for the Practice Company.

The Practice Company's accounts with balances have been entered in the CA-Simply general ledger. The Practice Company's trial balance is as follows:

**Practice Company**
**Trial Balance**
**September 15, 1992**

| | | |
|---|---|---|
| Cash | $ 4,000 | |
| Accounts Receivable | 11,000 | |
| Supplies | 800 | |
| Land | 18,600 | |
| Accounts Payable | | $ 3,000 |
| Tom Brown, Capital | | 29,000 |
| Tom Brown, Withdrawals | 1,200 | |
| Service Revenue | | 6,200 |
| Salary Expense | 1,600 | |
| Rent Expense | 800 | |
| Utilities Expense | 200 | |
| TOTAL | 38,200 | 38,200 |

**Working With the Practice Company**

To become familiar with CA-Simply Accounting, you can start the program and access the Practice Company data file on the data disk.

Place the data disk in the disk drive.

- Double click the Simply Accounting Icon.

A dialog box appears, with a list of data files and subdirectories.

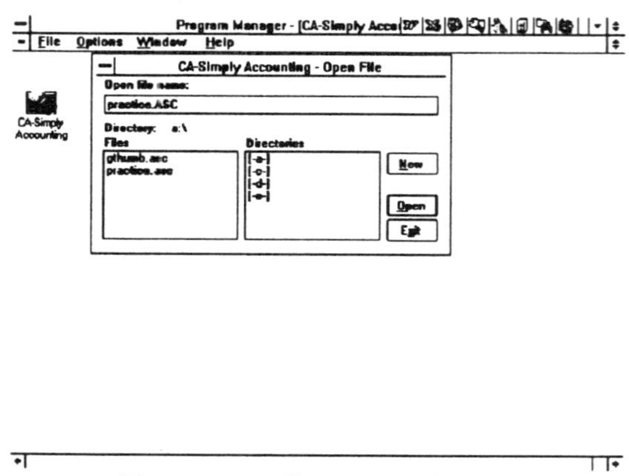


*Figure 1.1 Open Dialog Box*

- Double click the data drive location, [a] or [b].
- Double click Practice.ASC or TAB to the list to select Practice.ASC in the File Name list box and click Open.

Simply Accounting - Using Date dialog box displays. The Using Date is the date the program uses as the posting date for all journal entries made during the current session, unless you enter a different date with individual entries.

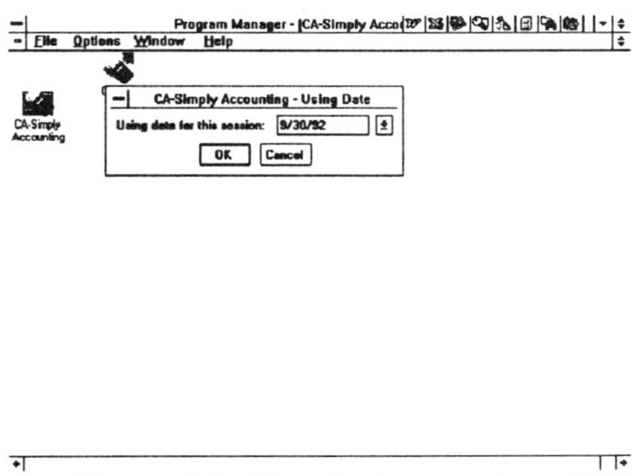


*Figure 1.2 Simply Accounting - Using Date*

- Enter **09/30/92** and click **OK**.

A dialog box displays informing you ***'The date entered is more than one week past your previous using date of 9/15/92''***. Click **OK**. The main window appears with the Practice Company name displayed in the title bar.

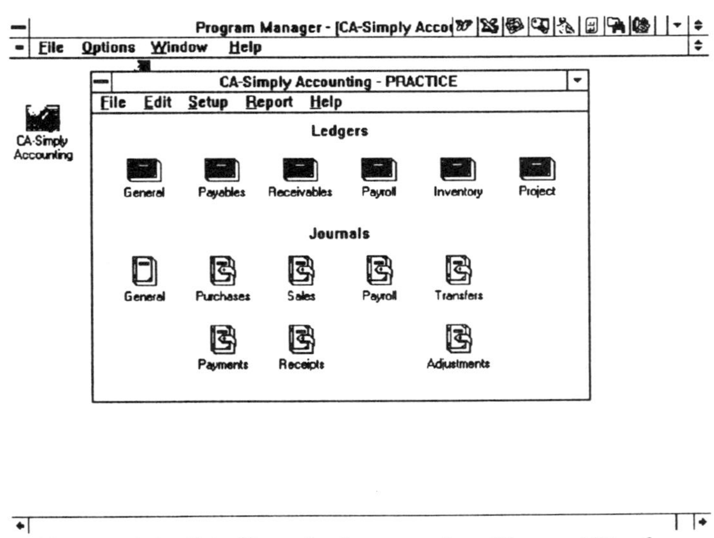


*Figure 1.3 CA-Simply Accounting Home Window*

**Journalizing Transactions**

Now that you've examined the trial balance, you are ready to journalize the following transactions.

To Access the Journal:

- Double click the General Journal Icon

  OR

- Click on **File** and Open Journal.

The journal screen displays:

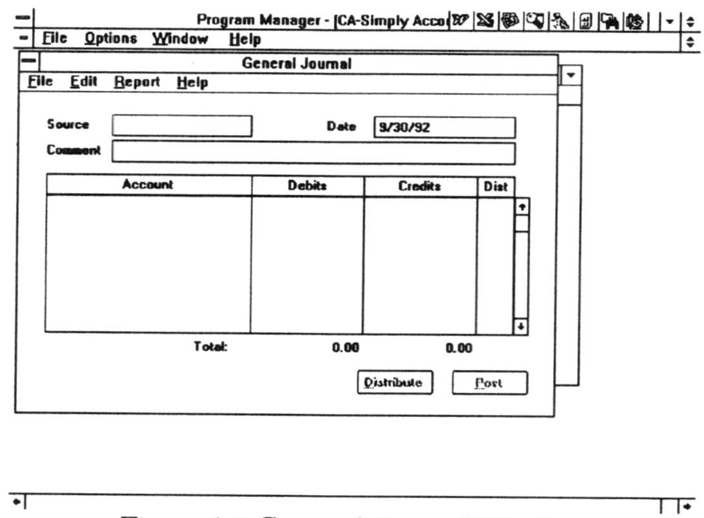


*Figure 1.4 General Journal Window*

To enter the following transaction in the journal, first manually record the journal entry in the space provided.

Sept. 15 Tom Brown collected $2,000 cash from a client for lawn services performed.

| *DATE* | *ACCT#* | *ACCOUNT NAME* | *DEBIT* | *CREDIT* |
|---|---|---|---|---|
| | | | | |
| | | | | |
| | | | | |
| | | | | |

*EXPLANATION:*

Record the entry using CA-Simply General Journal:

- Enter **GJ1** in the Source Field.
- Press **TAB** key to move to the Date Field.
- Enter **09/15/92** and press **TAB** key.
- Enter the description of the transaction:

  **Received cash on account from client.**
- Press **TAB** key.

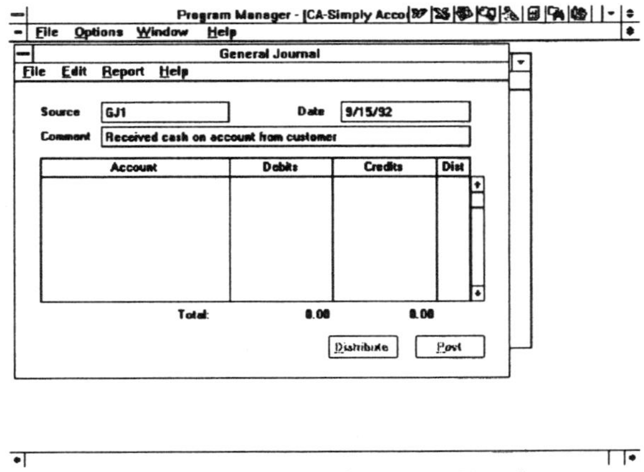


*Figure 1.5 Journal Entry Window*

- Press < **enter** > and the Select Account dialog box displays.

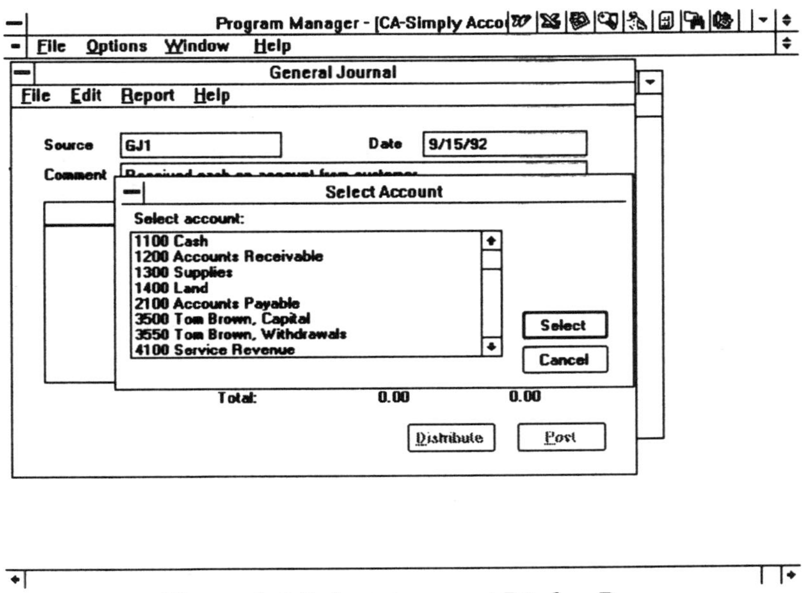


*Figure 1.6 Select Account Dialog Box*

- Select **Cash**.
- Enter **2,000.00** and press **TAB** key.
- Press < **enter** > .
- Select **Service Revenue** and press **TAB**.

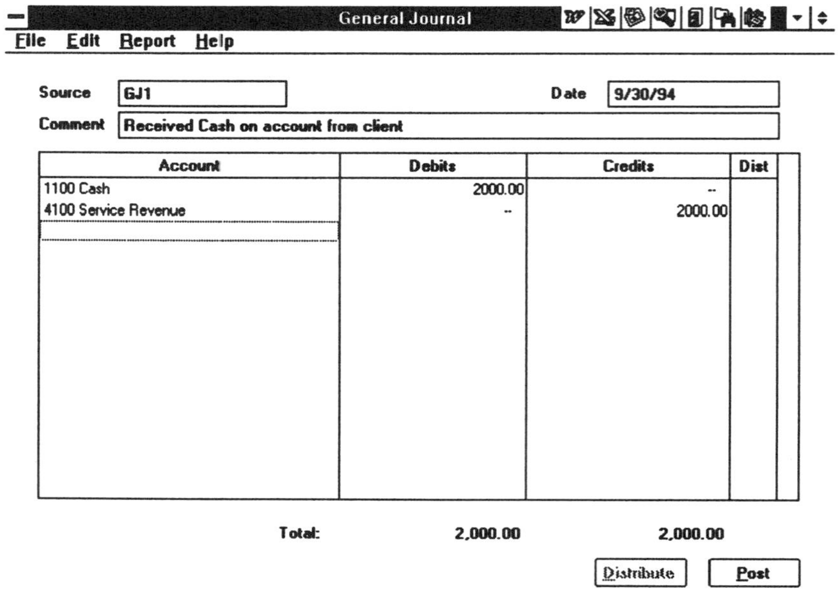


*Figure 1.7 Completed Journal Entry Window*

*To go back to any field on the journal screen, press the Shift key and Tab key.*

- Click the **POST** command button.

The transaction is complete and has been posted to the general ledger. Complete the remaining transactions, first by recording on the form provided and then in CA-Simply Accounting general journal. Remember to increment the source by one, GJ2, GJ3 and so on.

Sept. 16 Performed services for a client on account, $700.

| *DATE* | *ACCT#* | *ACCOUNT NAME* | *DEBIT* | *CREDIT* |
|---|---|---|---|---|
| | | | | |
| | | | | |
| | | | | |
| | | | | |

*EXPLANATION:*

Sept. 18 Paid utilities, $300.

| DATE | ACCT# | ACCOUNT NAME | DEBIT | CREDIT |
|---|---|---|---|---|
| | | | | |
| | | | | |
| | | | | |
| | | | | |

EXPLANATION:

Sept. 20 Paid on account, $1,000.

| DATE | ACCT# | ACCOUNT NAME | DEBIT | CREDIT |
|---|---|---|---|---|
| | | | | |
| | | | | |
| | | | | |
| | | | | |

EXPLANATION:

Sept. 21 Purchased supplies on account, $100.

| DATE | ACCT# | ACCOUNT NAME | DEBIT | CREDIT |
|---|---|---|---|---|
| | | | | |
| | | | | |
| | | | | |
| | | | | |

EXPLANATION:

Sept. 21 Withdrew $1,200 for personal use.

| DATE | ACCT# | ACCOUNT NAME | DEBIT | CREDIT |
|---|---|---|---|---|
| | | | | |
| | | | | |
| | | | | |
| | | | | |

EXPLANATION:

Sept. 21 Performed services for $4,400 on account.

| *DATE* | *ACCT#* | *ACCOUNT NAME* | *DEBIT* | *CREDIT* |
|---|---|---|---|---|
| | | | | |
| | | | | |
| | | | | |
| | | | | |

*EXPLANATION:*

Sept. 22 Received cash of $2,000 for audit work just completed.

| *DATE* | *ACCT#* | *ACCOUNT NAME* | *DEBIT* | *CREDIT* |
|---|---|---|---|---|
| | | | | |
| | | | | |
| | | | | |
| | | | | |

*EXPLANATION:*

Sept. 28 Paid rent, $800.

| *DATE* | *ACCT#* | *ACCOUNT NAME* | *DEBIT* | *CREDIT* |
|---|---|---|---|---|
| | | | | |
| | | | | |
| | | | | |
| | | | | |

*EXPLANATION:*

Sept. 30 Paid employees' salaries, $1600.

| *DATE* | *ACCT#* | *ACCOUNT NAME* | *DEBIT* | *CREDIT* |
|---|---|---|---|---|
| | | | | |
| | | | | |
| | | | | |
| | | | | |

*EXPLANATION:*

CA-Simply posts each entry as it is completed. If an entry is entered incorrectly and you have posted the entry, you may correct the entry by entering a correcting entry or reversing the original entry and re-enter the correct entry.

**Printing Reports**

When all entries have been entered, from the Main menu, click Report from the menu bar and select the report to print. The reports to print are

- General Journal
- Trial Balance
- General Ledger
- Balance Sheet
- Income Statement

**To print:**

- Click on each Report name.
- Click **File**.
- Click **Print** to send to the printer.
- Close the Report window.

## Backing Up Data Files

Backup of data files is a very important step in the computerized accounting system. In the computerized system, when you post your transactions, the financial statements are automatically updated. To save any activity prior to posting or after posting, you can do a backup of your data files. Another use for the backup of data files would be to allow you to go back to a previous session's work, if necessary. You can copy your backup files to your working disk, and make any changes. Keep in mind that, when this is done, you will lose any work done prior to this session. The restoring of backup files will replace the existing files. When to do backups will be indicated in the practice sets.

**Making A Backup Copy**

Use File Manager to make a copy of the data disk. Keep two disks to ensure backup of your data files. From the Program Manager:

- Click **Main**.
- Click **File Manager**.
- Click **Disk** from the menu.
- Click **Copy Disk**.
- Place the data disk in the disk drive as your source disk.

Follow the instructions on the screen to prompt you for the destination disk.

- Replace the source disk with destination disk.
- Click **OK**.

When the copy is made, close File Manager window. Label the disks appropriately.

## Exiting CA-Simply

After completing the transactions and printing all reports, you should exit CA-Simply.

**To Exit CA-Simply:**

Click the Control menu bar in the upper left corner OR
Click **File**, then Click **Exit**.

## Chapter Summary

After completing this chapter, you were able to compare the manual system to a computerized system, access Practice Company files, enter transactions, print reports and make a backup copy of your data files. In Chapter 2, you will work with a sole proprietorship company and record transactions completing the accounting cycle.

# Chapter 2

# The Greenthumb Landscaping Service

## Overview

In this chapter, you will begin to work with the CA-Simply General Ledger module to enter the September business transactions for The Greenthumb, a landscaping business. First, you will enter the transactions in the forms provided throughout the chapter. Once you have analyzed and entered the transactions manually and are certain that they are correct, you can enter them in the CA-Simply program. You will print out a trial balance, make adjusting entries, and print financial statements. Before you complete this chapter, you will manually balance the accounts receivable and accounts payable subsidiary ledgers on the forms provided. This practice set is best implemented after completing the adjusting entry chapter of your accounting textbook.

## Objectives

After working through this chapter, you will be able to:

1. Access Greenthumb Landscaping Services using CA-Simply.
2. Enter transactions in the General Journal.
3. Print the Trial Balance.
4. Enter Adjusting Entries.
5. Print the Financial Statements.
6. Balance the subsidiary ledgers, accounts receivable and accounts payable.
7. Backup data files.
8. Exit CA-Simply.

**The Greenthumb Landscaping Service**
Matthew Weed owns and operates The Greenthumb, a landscaping business. It is a sole proprietorship service company.

The company's accounting system is based on a calendar year. On September 1, 1992, the existing accounts numbers, account names and their balances for the company are shown in the trial balance below. Subsidiary balance information for customers and vendors are given as well.

The Greenthumb Landscaping Service
Trial Balance
September 1, 1992

| | | | |
|---|---|---|---|
| 1100 | Cash | $ 9,140 | |
| 1200 | Accounts Receivable | 13,200 | |
| 1300 | Supplies | 3,150 | |
| 1400 | Prepaid Insurance | 3,600 | |
| 1500 | Notes Receivable, Long-Term | 10,000 | |
| 1600 | Lawn Equipment | 18,530 | |
| 1650 | Accum. Dep. Lawn Equipment | | $ 6,250 |
| 2100 | Accounts Payable | | 9,200 |
| 2200 | Salary Payable | | 300 |
| 2300 | Notes Payable, Current | | |
| 2400 | Interest Payable | | 250 |
| 2500 | Unearned Service Revenue | | |
| 2600 | Note Payable, Long-Term | | 13,600 |
| 3750 | Capital, Matthew Weed | | 28,020 |
| 3760 | Withdrawals, Matthew Weed | | |
| 4100 | Service Revenue | | |
| 4200 | Interest Revenue | | |
| 5100 | Salary Expense | | |
| 5200 | Rent Expense | | |
| 5300 | Depreciation Expense | | |
| 5400 | Insurance Expense | | |
| 5500 | Utilities Expense | | |
| 5600 | Supplies Expense | | |
| 5700 | Interest Expense | | |
| | Total | 57,620 | 57,620 |

Before entering the transactions into the CA-Simply accounting system, you should print the trial balance to be sure it corresponds with the trial balance displayed. From the main menu,

- Click **Report**.
- Click **Trial Balance**.
- Click **OK** for the date.

- Click **File**.
- Click **Print**.

Close the Trial Balance window.

**Subsidiary Account Information**
On August 31, 1992, the amount of accounts receivable outstanding was $13,200 from the following customers:

| | |
|---|---|
| J. Williams | $ 600 |
| Joan Towne | 4,500 |
| T.C. Homecare | 3,000 |
| R.S. Topsoil | 5,100 |
| Tim Rose | 000 |
| W.D. Clamp | 000 |

The accounts payable owing on August 31, 1992 was $9,200 and was payable to the following vendors:

| | |
|---|---|
| ABC Nursery | $ 1,000 |
| J & J Equipment | 6,000 |
| A.J. Business Forms | 500 |
| Oak Nursery | 1,100 |
| Desks & ETC | 100 |
| N.E. Hardware | 500 |

Manually set up the balances on the forms given at the end of the chapter. Enter the beginning balances and post any transactions as they occur for each customer or vendor.

## Accessing The Greenthumb Landscaping Service Using CA-Simply

To begin a session using CA-Simply, you will place the data disk containing the Greenthumb company files in the disk drive. The accounts have been entered with beginning balances. A list of transactions follow to be recorded in the general journal. After completing the journalizing, you will print the trial balance for Greenthumb Company.

**Working With the Greenthumb Landscaping Company**
To become familiar with CA-Simply Accounting, you can start the program and access the Greenthumb Company data file on the data disk.

Place the data disk in the disk drive.

- Double click the Simply Accounting Icon.

CA dialog box appears, with a list of data files and subdirectories in which you installed CA-Simply Accounting.

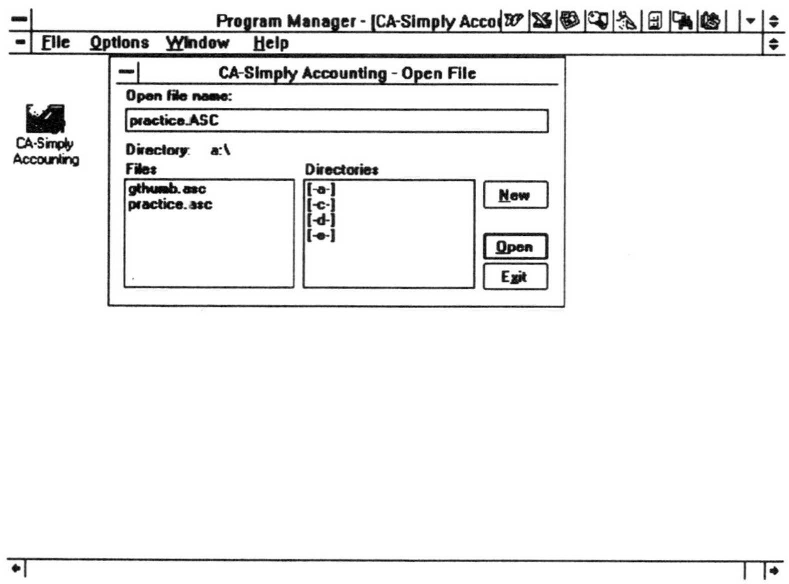


*Figure 2.1 Open File Dialog Box*

- Double click the data drive location, [a] or [b]..
- Double click **GTHUMB.ASC** or **TAB** to the list to select **GTHUMB.ASC** in the File Name list box and Click **Open**.

Simply Accounting - Using Date dialog box displays. The Using Date is the date the program uses as the posting date for all journal entries made during the current session, unless you enter a different date with individual entries.

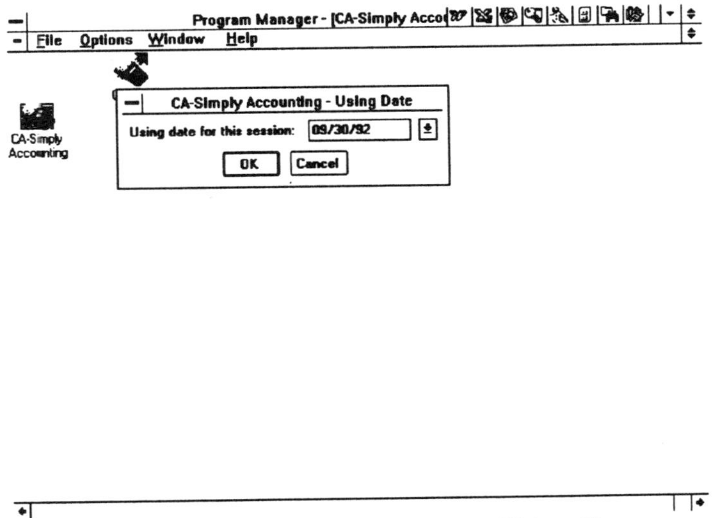


*Figure 2.2 Simply Accounting - Using Date*

- Enter **09/30/92** and click **OK**.

The main window appears with the Practice Company name displayed in the title bar.

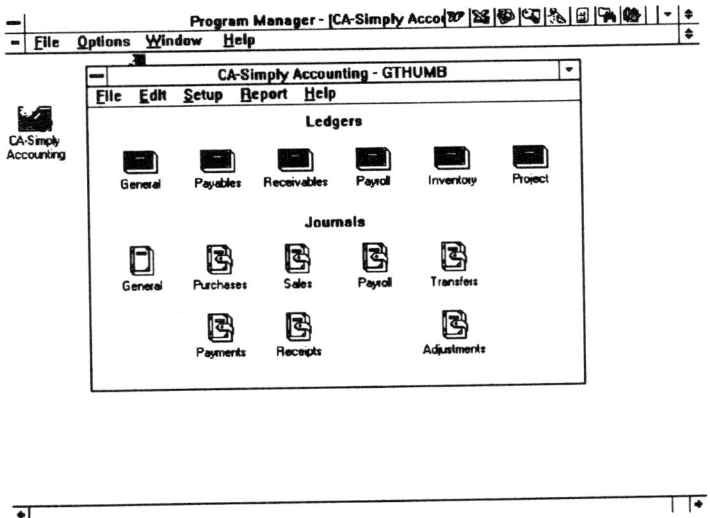


*Figure 2.3 CA-Simply Accounting Home Window*

**Printing The Chart of Accounts**

From the main or general ledger window:

- Single click General Ledger Icon from the Main Window.
- Click **Report** from the menu bar.

- Select Display Chart Of Accounts.

The Chart of Accounts displays.

- Click **File**.
- Click **Print**.
- Close the Chart of Accounts window.

**Printing the Trial Balance**
Before entering the transactions, print a trial balance.

- Click **Report** from the menu bar.
- Select Trial Balance.
- Enter **09/01/92** and click **OK**.

The Trial Balance displays.
**To Print:**

- Click **File**.
- Click **Print**.
- Close the Trial Balance window.

## Journalizing Transactions

Now that you've examined the trial balance, you are ready to journalize the following transactions for the month of September.

To Access the General Journal:

- Double click the General Journal Icon OR Click **File**, then click **Open Journal**.

The journal screen displays.

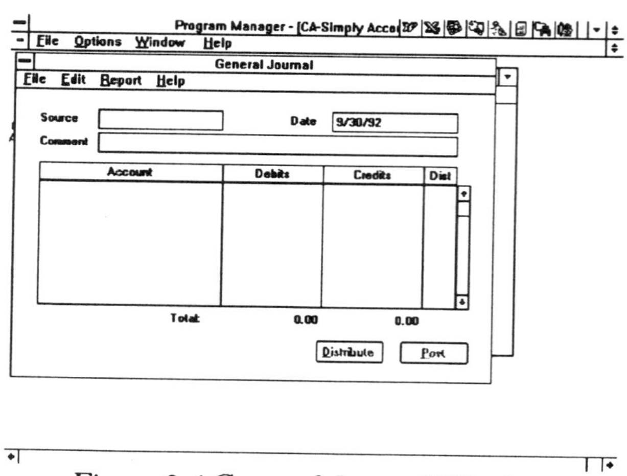


*Figure 2.4 General Journal Window*

Manually record the journal entry on the form provided and then enter the entry in the CA-Simply Accounting general journal.

The first entry is as follows:
Sept. 1 Performed lawn service for J. Williams and received $100.00.

| *DATE* | *ACCT#* | *ACCOUNT NAME* | *DEBIT* | *CREDIT* |
|---|---|---|---|---|
| | | | | |
| | | | | |
| | | | | |
| | | | | |

*EXPLANATION:*

Record the first entry using CA-Simply General Journal:

- Enter **GJ1** in the Source Field.
- Press **TAB** key to move to the Date field.
- Enter **09/01/92** and press **TAB** key.
- Enter the description of the transaction:

  **Performed lawn services for J. Williams**.
- Press **TAB** key.

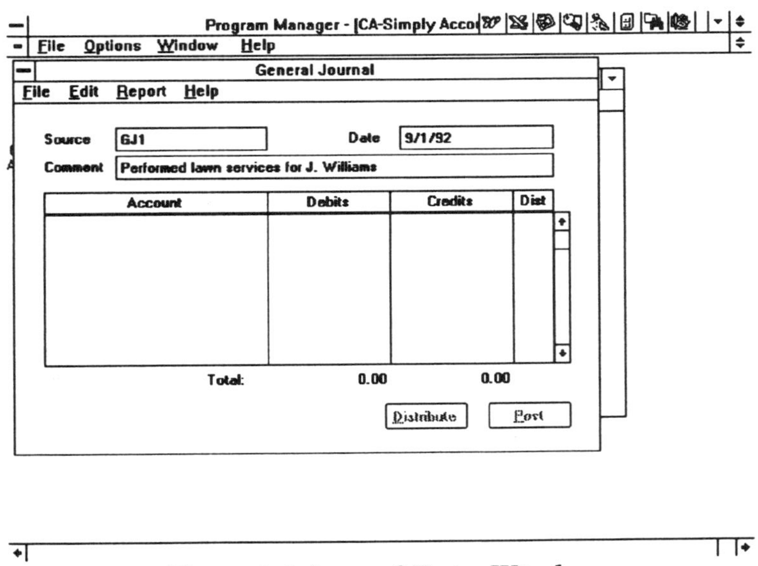


*Figure 2.5 Journal Entry Window*

- Press < **enter** > and the Select Account dialog box displays.

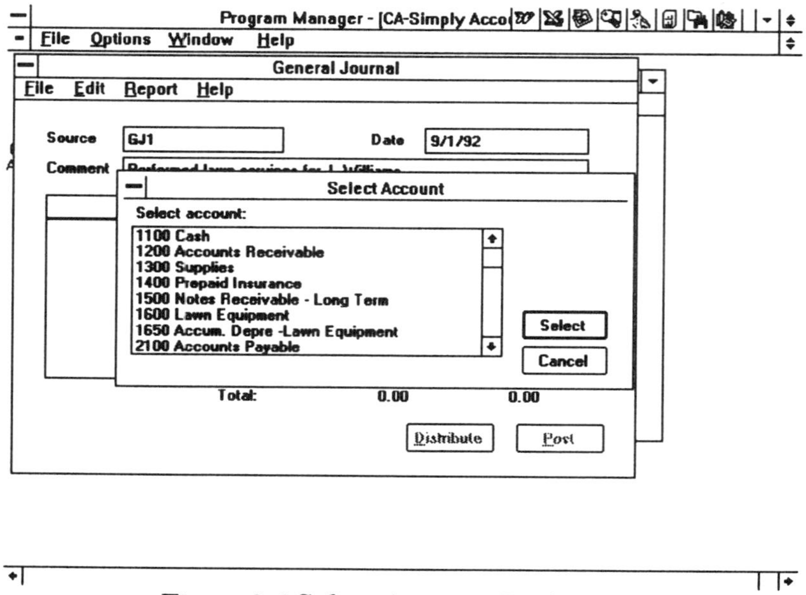


*Figure 2.6 Select Account Dialog Box*

- Select **Cash** and press < **enter** > .
- Enter **100.00** and press **TAB** key.
- Press < **enter** > .
- Select **Service Revenue** and press < **enter** > .

  The same amount in the debit column appears in the credit column. If the amount is different, enter the new amount.
- Press **Tab**. (Press the **Shift** + **Tab** key to go back to any fields to make changes.)

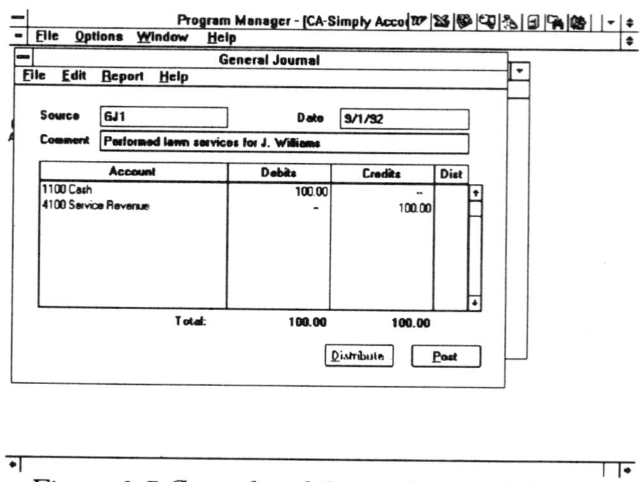


*Figure 2.7 Completed Journal Entry Window*

- Click the **POST** command button.

The transaction is complete and has been posted to the general ledger. Complete the remaining transactions, first by recording on the form provided and then in CA-Simply Accounting general journal. Remember to increment the source by one, GJ2,GJ3 and so on.

Sept. 1 Purchased supplies on credit from ABC Nursery, $500.00.

| *DATE* | *ACCT#* | *ACCOUNT NAME* | *DEBIT* | *CREDIT* |
|---|---|---|---|---|
| | | | | |
| | | | | |
| | | | | |
| | | | | |

*EXPLANATION:*

Sept. 1 Purchased lawn equipment from J & J Equipment, for $10,000; signed a note payable for $ 8,000 and issued a check no. 101 for $2,000.

| *DATE* | *ACCT#* | *ACCOUNT NAME* | *DEBIT* | *CREDIT* |
|---|---|---|---|---|
| | | | | |
| | | | | |
| | | | | |
| | | | | |

*EXPLANATION:*

Sept. 1 Received check no. 784 from R. S. Topsoil for August 31 balance on his account.

| *DATE* | *ACCT#* | *ACCOUNT NAME* | *DEBIT* | *CREDIT* |
|---|---|---|---|---|
| | | | | |
| | | | | |
| | | | | |
| | | | | |

*EXPLANATION:*

Sept. 4 Issued check no. 102 to pay salaries of $1250.00, which included Salary Payable of $300.00 from August 31.

| DATE | ACCT# | ACCOUNT NAME | DEBIT | CREDIT |
| --- | --- | --- | --- | --- |
| | | | | |
| | | | | |
| | | | | |
| | | | | |

EXPLANATION:

Sept. 4 Issued invoice no. 401 to Joan Towne for services on account, $1,350.00.

| DATE | ACCT# | ACCOUNT NAME | DEBIT | CREDIT |
| --- | --- | --- | --- | --- |
| | | | | |
| | | | | |
| | | | | |
| | | | | |

*EXPLANATION:*

Sept. 4 Issued check no. 103 for September rent of $2500.00.

| DATE | ACCT# | ACCOUNT NAME | DEBIT | CREDIT |
| --- | --- | --- | --- | --- |
| | | | | |
| | | | | |
| | | | | |
| | | | | |

*EXPLANATION:*

Sept. 8 Purchased supplies from A.J. Business Forms, $425.00, on account.

| DATE | ACCT# | ACCOUNT NAME | DEBIT | CREDIT |
| --- | --- | --- | --- | --- |
| | | | | |
| | | | | |
| | | | | |
| | | | | |

*EXPLANATION:*

Sept. 8 Issued invoice no. 402 to W.D. Clamp for lawn service, $3,500.00.

| *DATE* | *ACCT#* | *ACCOUNT NAME* | *DEBIT* | *CREDIT* |
|---|---|---|---|---|
| | | | | |
| | | | | |
| | | | | |
| | | | | |

*EXPLANATION:*

Sept. 8 Issued invoice no. 403 to Tim Rose for lawn services, $2250.00.

| *DATE* | *ACCT#* | *ACCOUNT NAME* | *DEBIT* | *CREDIT* |
|---|---|---|---|---|
| | | | | |
| | | | | |
| | | | | |
| | | | | |

*EXPLANATION:*

Sept. 11 Issued check no. 104 to pay Oak Nursery the amount owed on August 31, $1,100.

| *DATE* | *ACCT#* | *ACCOUNT NAME* | *DEBIT* | *CREDIT* |
|---|---|---|---|---|
| | | | | |
| | | | | |
| | | | | |
| | | | | |

*EXPLANATION:*

Sept. 11 Received $550.00 in advance from W.D. Clamp for a two month lawn contract.

| *DATE* | *ACCT#* | *ACCOUNT NAME* | *DEBIT* | *CREDIT* |
|---|---|---|---|---|
| | | | | |
| | | | | |
| | | | | |
| | | | | |

*EXPLANATION:*

Sept. 11 Issued check no. 105 to pay ABC Nursery the amount from Sept. 1 purchase.

| DATE | ACCT# | ACCOUNT NAME | DEBIT | CREDIT |
|---|---|---|---|---|
| | | | | |
| | | | | |
| | | | | |
| | | | | |

EXPLANATION:

Sept. 11 Received payment of $1,000.00 from Joan Towne on account.

| DATE | ACCT# | ACCOUNT NAME | DEBIT | CREDIT |
|---|---|---|---|---|
| | | | | |
| | | | | |
| | | | | |
| | | | | |

EXPLANATION:

Sept. 18 Purchased supplies on credit from Oak Nursery for $200.00.

| DATE | ACCT# | ACCOUNT NAME | DEBIT | CREDIT |
|---|---|---|---|---|
| | | | | |
| | | | | |
| | | | | |
| | | | | |

EXPLANATION:

Sept. 18 Purchased lawn equipment on credit from J & J Equipment, $4000.00.

| DATE | ACCT# | ACCOUNT NAME | DEBIT | CREDIT |
|---|---|---|---|---|
| | | | | |
| | | | | |
| | | | | |
| | | | | |

EXPLANATION:

Sept. 18 Issued check no. 106 to pay salaries, $2250.00.

| *DATE* | *ACCT#* | *ACCOUNT NAME* | *DEBIT* | *CREDIT* |
|---|---|---|---|---|
| | | | | |
| | | | | |
| | | | | |
| | | | | |

*EXPLANATION:*

Sept. 18 Issued invoice no. 404 to T.C. Homecare for services, $2,800.00.

| *DATE* | *ACCT#* | *ACCOUNT NAME* | *DEBIT* | *CREDIT* |
|---|---|---|---|---|
| | | | | |
| | | | | |
| | | | | |
| | | | | |

*EXPLANATION:*

Sept. 20 Received check no. 212 from Tim Rose for the amount from Sept. 8.

| *DATE* | *ACCT#* | *ACCOUNT NAME* | *DEBIT* | *CREDIT* |
|---|---|---|---|---|
| | | | | |
| | | | | |
| | | | | |
| | | | | |

*EXPLANATION:*

Sept. 20 Issued check no. 107 for $190.00 to pay utilities.

| *DATE* | *ACCT#* | *ACCOUNT NAME* | *DEBIT* | *CREDIT* |
|---|---|---|---|---|
| | | | | |
| | | | | |
| | | | | |
| | | | | |

*EXPLANATION:*

Sept. 20 Purchased supplies on credit from Desks & ETC., $125.00.

| DATE | ACCT# | ACCOUNT NAME | DEBIT | CREDIT |
|---|---|---|---|---|
| | | | | |
| | | | | |
| | | | | |
| | | | | |

*EXPLANATION:*

Sept. 20 Issued invoice no. 405 to R.S. Topsoil for services rendered, $300.00

| DATE | ACCT# | ACCOUNT NAME | DEBIT | CREDIT |
|---|---|---|---|---|
| | | | | |
| | | | | |
| | | | | |
| | | | | |

*EXPLANATION:*

Sept. 25 Received $1,250.00 on account from W.D. Clamp.

| DATE | ACCT# | ACCOUNT NAME | DEBIT | CREDIT |
|---|---|---|---|---|
| | | | | |
| | | | | |
| | | | | |
| | | | | |

*EXPLANATION:*

Sept. 25 Performed services for cash customers, $1,500.00.

| DATE | ACCT# | ACCOUNT NAME | DEBIT | CREDIT |
|---|---|---|---|---|
| | | | | |
| | | | | |
| | | | | |
| | | | | |

*EXPLANATION:*

Sept. 30 Purchased supplies on account N.E. Hardware, $215.00.

| *DATE* | *ACCT#* | *ACCOUNT NAME* | *DEBIT* | *CREDIT* |
|---|---|---|---|---|
| | | | | |
| | | | | |
| | | | | |
| | | | | |

*EXPLANATION:*

Sept. 30 Collected interest revenue, $1000.00.

| *DATE* | *ACCT#* | *ACCOUNT NAME* | *DEBIT* | *CREDIT* |
|---|---|---|---|---|
| | | | | |
| | | | | |
| | | | | |
| | | | | |

*EXPLANATION:*

Sept. 30 Issued check no. 108 to Matthew Weed, owner of the business, for personal use, $250.00.

| *DATE* | *ACCT#* | *ACCOUNT NAME* | *DEBIT* | *CREDIT* |
|---|---|---|---|---|
| | | | | |
| | | | | |
| | | | | |
| | | | | |

*EXPLANATION:*

After all transactions are completed, exit the journal.

## Printing the Trial Balance

Once all entries are recorded and posted, you should print the trial balance.

- Click **Report** from the menu bar.
- Select Trial Balance.
- Enter **09/30/92**.

The Trial Balance displays.
To Print:

- Click **File**.
- Click **Print**.
- Close the Trial Balance window.

- Repeat the steps above to print the General Journal and General Ledger.

## Entering Adjusting Entries

Once the trial balance has been printed, make the following adjusting entries. Then, enter the adjustments in the general journal. Enter ADJ1, ADJ2, and so on for the source.

**Adjusting Entries:**
Sept. 30 Accrued Interest Expense $125.00

| *DATE* | *ACCT#* | *ACCOUNT NAME* | *DEBIT* | *CREDIT* |
|---|---|---|---|---|
| | | | | |
| | | | | |
| | | | | |
| | | | | |

*EXPLANATION:*

Sept. 30 Supplies on Hand $125.00

| *DATE* | *ACCT#* | *ACCOUNT NAME* | *DEBIT* | *CREDIT* |
|---|---|---|---|---|
| | | | | |
| | | | | |
| | | | | |
| | | | | |

*EXPLANATION:*

Sept. 30 The balance in Prepaid Insurance reflects 12 months. Record the expired insurance for September.

| *DATE* | *ACCT#* | *ACCOUNT NAME* | *DEBIT* | *CREDIT* |
|---|---|---|---|---|
| | | | | |
| | | | | |
| | | | | |
| | | | | |

*EXPLANATION:*

Sept. 30 Depreciation Expense Lawn Equipment, $200.00

| *DATE* | *ACCT#* | *ACCOUNT NAME* | *DEBIT* | *CREDIT* |
|---|---|---|---|---|
| | | | | |
| | | | | |
| | | | | |
| | | | | |

*EXPLANATION:*

Sept. 30 Accrued Salary Expense, $750.00

| *DATE* | *ACCT#* | *ACCOUNT NAME* | *DEBIT* | *CREDIT* |
|---|---|---|---|---|
| | | | | |
| | | | | |
| | | | | |
| | | | | |

*EXPLANATION:*

Sept. 30 At the end of the month, the balance in the Unearned Revenue account has a balance of $250.

| *DATE* | *ACCT#* | *ACCOUNT NAME* | *DEBIT* | *CREDIT* |
|---|---|---|---|---|
| | | | | |
| | | | | |
| | | | | |
| | | | | |

*EXPLANATION:*

CA-Simply posts each entry as it is completed. If an entry is entered incorrectly and you have posted the entry, you may correct the posted entry by entering a correcting entry and then enter the correct entry.

## Printing the Financial Statements

Once all adjusting entries are recorded and posted, you should print the trial balance and the financial reports.

Printing Reports

When all entries have been entered, Click **Report** from the menu bar and select the report to print. The reports to print are

- General Journal
- Trial Balance
- General Ledger

- Balance Sheet
- Income Statement

To print:

- Click on each Report name.
- Enter the date and click **OK**.
- Click **File**.
- Click **Print** to send to the printer.
- Close the Report window.

## Balancing the Subsidiary Ledgers Against the General Ledger

You must now ensure that the total amount of the customer accounts in the accounts receivable and accounts payable subsidiary ledgers agree with their respective balances in the general ledger. You will do this manually, since the accounts receivable and accounts payable modules in CA-Simply were not activated to automatically update the customer and vendor accounts. Use the subsidiary ledger forms provided below to prepare a manual balance of the subsidiary ledgers and compare the balances to the respective control accounts in the general ledger.

**Customer:**

| Date | Description | Dr. | Cr. | Balance |
|---|---|---|---|---|
| | Opening Balance | | | |
| | | | | |
| | | | | |
| | | | | |
| | | | | |
| | | | | |
| | | | | |
| | | | | |
| | | | | |
| | | | | |

| Customer: | | | | |
|---|---|---|---|---|
| Date | Description | Dr. | Cr. | Balance |
| | Opening Balance | | | |
| | | | | |
| | | | | |
| | | | | |
| | | | | |
| | | | | |
| | | | | |
| | | | | |
| | | | | |
| | | | | |

| Customer: | | | | |
|---|---|---|---|---|
| Date | Description | Dr. | Cr. | Balance |
| | Opening Balance | | | |
| | | | | |
| | | | | |
| | | | | |
| | | | | |
| | | | | |
| | | | | |
| | | | | |
| | | | | |
| | | | | |

| Customer: | | | | |
|---|---|---|---|---|
| Date | Description | Dr. | Cr. | Balance |
| | Opening Balance | | | |
| | | | | |
| | | | | |
| | | | | |
| | | | | |
| | | | | |
| | | | | |
| | | | | |
| | | | | |
| | | | | |

| Customer: | | | | |
|---|---|---|---|---|
| Date | Description | Dr. | Cr. | Balance |
| | Opening Balance | | | |
| | | | | |
| | | | | |
| | | | | |
| | | | | |
| | | | | |
| | | | | |
| | | | | |
| | | | | |
| | | | | |

| Customer: | | | | |
|---|---|---|---|---|
| **Date** | **Description** | **Dr.** | **Cr.** | **Balance** |
| | Opening Balance | | | |
| | | | | |
| | | | | |
| | | | | |
| | | | | |
| | | | | |
| | | | | |
| | | | | |
| | | | | |
| | | | | |

| Vendor: | | | | |
|---|---|---|---|---|
| **Date** | **Description** | **Dr.** | **Cr.** | **Balance** |
| | Opening Balance | | | |
| | | | | |
| | | | | |
| | | | | |
| | | | | |
| | | | | |
| | | | | |
| | | | | |
| | | | | |
| | | | | |

Vendor:

| Date | Description | Dr. | Cr. | Balance |
|---|---|---|---|---|
| | Opening Balance | | | |
| | | | | |
| | | | | |
| | | | | |
| | | | | |
| | | | | |
| | | | | |
| | | | | |
| | | | | |
| | | | | |

Vendor:

| Date | Description | Dr. | Cr. | Balance |
|---|---|---|---|---|
| | Opening Balance | | | |
| | | | | |
| | | | | |
| | | | | |
| | | | | |
| | | | | |
| | | | | |
| | | | | |
| | | | | |
| | | | | |

| Vendor: | | | | |
|---|---|---|---|---|
| Date | Description | Dr. | Cr. | Balance |
| | Opening Balance | | | |
| | | | | |
| | | | | |
| | | | | |
| | | | | |
| | | | | |
| | | | | |
| | | | | |
| | | | | |
| | | | | |

| Vendor: | | | | |
|---|---|---|---|---|
| Date | Description | Dr. | Cr. | Balance |
| | Opening Balance | | | |
| | | | | |
| | | | | |
| | | | | |
| | | | | |
| | | | | |
| | | | | |
| | | | | |
| | | | | |
| | | | | |

| Vendor: | | | | |
|---|---|---|---|---|
| Date | Description | Dr. | Cr. | Balance |
| | Opening Balance | | | |
| | | | | |
| | | | | |
| | | | | |
| | | | | |
| | | | | |
| | | | | |
| | | | | |
| | | | | |
| | | | | |

## Backing Up Data Files

Backup of data files is a very important step in the computerized accounting system. In the computerized system, when you post your transactions, the financial statements are automatically updated. To save any activity prior to posting or after posting, you can do a backup of your data files. Another use for the backup of data files would be to allow you to go back to a previous session's work, if necessary. You can copy your backup files to your working disk, and make any changes. Keep in mind that, when this is done, you will lose any work done prior to this session. The restoring of backup files will replace the existing files. When to do backups will be indicated in the practice sets.

**Making A Backup Copy**

Use File Manager to make a copy of the data disk. Keep two disks to ensure backup of your data files. From the Program Manager:

- Click **Main**.
- Click **File Manager**.
- Click **Disk** from the menu.
- Click **Copy Disk**.
- Place the data disk in the disk drive as your source disk.

Follow the instructions on the screen to prompt you for the destination disk.

- Replace the source disk with destination disk.
- Click **OK**.

When the copy is made, close File Manager window. Label the disks appropriately.

## CA-Simply Accounting Close

CA-Simply Accounting continues to the next month's transaction by the Using Date entered. The program automatically closes the year when you enter a date beyond the ending fiscal date as the Using Date. You have completed the accounting cycle for CA-Simply Accounting.

## Exiting CA-Simply

After completing the transactions and printing all reports, you should exit CA-Simply.

**To Exit CA-Simply:**

Click the Control menu bar in the upper left corner OR
Click **File**, then Click **Exit**.

## Chapter Summary

In this chapter, you have completed the accounting cycle, entering transactions in the general ledger, printing financial reports, and backing up the data files for a service company. Chapter 3 will work with a sales and service company and require the complete setup of accounts and balances for Krystal's Boutique before entering transactions for the month.

# Chapter 3

## Krystal's Boutique
## Sales And Service Company-
## The General Ledger

### Overview

This chapter will allow you to work with the CA-Simply Accounting system in more detail. You will set up the data files for Krystal's Boutique. You will assume that you are converting from a manual accounting system to the CA-Simply system. This requires entering the chart of accounts with their respective initial balances. This practice set should be done after completing the merchandising chapter in your accounting textbook.

### Objectives

After completing this chapter, you will be able to:

1. Enter a new company and new company information.
2. Construct the Chart of Accounts.
3. Print the Chart of Accounts.
4. Initialize account balances.
5. Print a Trial Balance.
6. Exit CA-Simply.

### Entering New Company ID and Company Information

Krystal's Boutique is both a sales and service corporation, and uses the **periodic inventory method**. The company's accounting cycle is based on a calendar year. To begin a session using CA-Simply, you will place the data disk in the disk drive. You will enter the chart of accounts with initial balances displayed in the financial statements in Figures 3.1 and 3.2.

***Place the data disk in the disk drive.***

- Double click the CA- Simply Accounting Icon.

A dialog box appears, with a list of data files and subdirectories.

- Click the data drive location, [a] or [b].

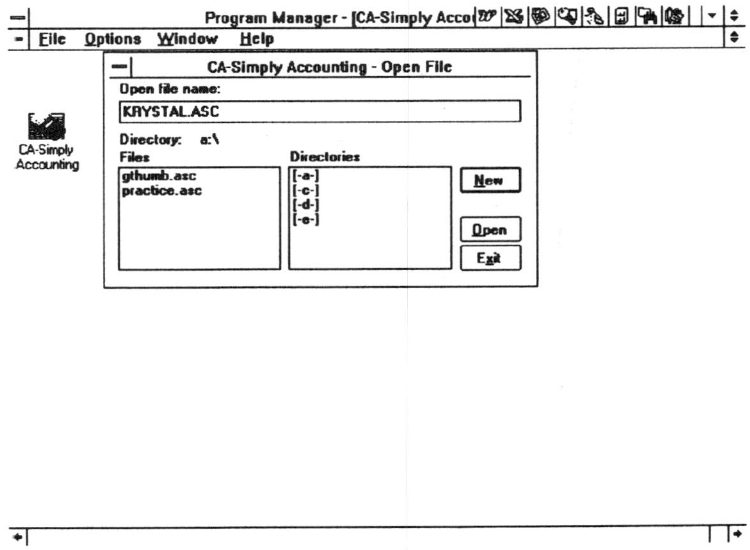


*Figure 3.1 Open File Dialog Box*

- Enter **KRYSTAL** in the file name box.
- Click **NEW**.

CA-Simply Accounting displays the Company Dates dialog box.

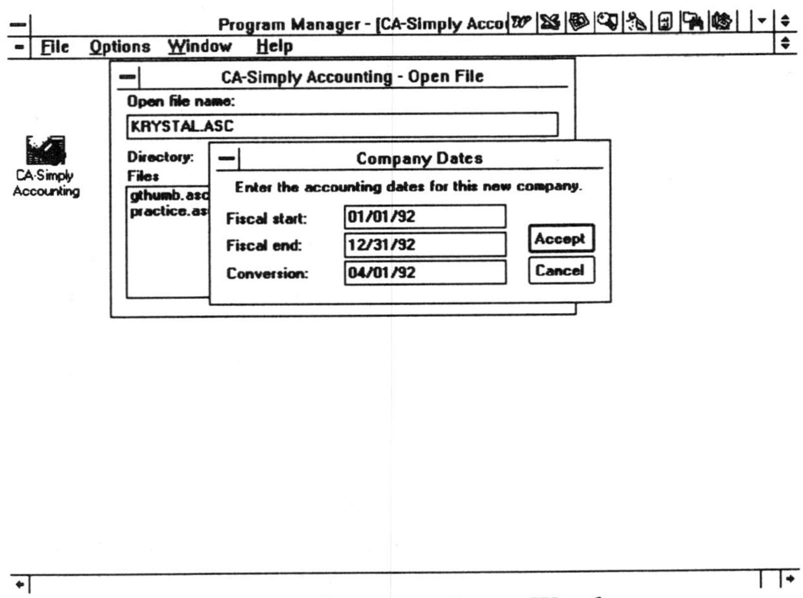


*Figure 3.2 Company Dates Window*

- Enter **01/01/92** for the Fiscal Start date.
- Press the TAB key.
- Enter **12/31/92** for the Fiscal End date.
- Press the **TAB** key.
- Enter **04/01/92** for the Conversion date.
- Click the **Accept** button.

The main window appears with Krystal displayed in the title bar. To enter the company information below,

- Click **Setup** from the menu bar.
- Click **Company Information**.

Enter the following data:

**Krystal's Boutique**
**1412 Rodeo Drive**
**Beverly Hills, CA 90210**

Notice the Fiscal Start, Fiscal End and the Conversion date display to the right of the screen.

- Click **OK** to accept the information.

## Constructing the Chart of Accounts

The financial statements for Krystal's Boutique are given in Figures 3.4 and 3.5. When entering the chart of accounts, you will need an account number, account name, account balance and account type. Next to each account name is an account type, designated as:

| | |
|---|---|
| **H** | **Block Heading** |
| **L** | **Left Column** |
| **R** | **Right Column** |
| **S** | **Subtotal** |
| **T** | **Block total** |

The designation of Left and Right type accounts does not equate to debit and credit. Left and right type reflect the position the account balance will print on the financial statement. If you use left type accounts, then each group must have an S type for a subtotal and a T type for total. If you use right type accounts then each group uses a T type for total without an S type for subtotal. CA-Simply Accounting requires all balances to be entered as positive amounts unless the account reflects a contra balance. For example, Accumulated Depreciation is a contra asset and maintains a credit balance, therefore you would enter the balance as a negative amount.

Be sure to number the accounts in the financial statements. CA-Simply accounting uses the following numbering system:

| | |
|---|---|
| **1000-1999** | **Assets** |
| **2000-2999** | **Liabilities** |
| **3000-3999** | **Equity** |
| **4000-4999** | **Revenue** |
| **5000-5999** | **Expenses** |

## Entering the Chart of Accounts

The financial statements in figure 3.4 and 3.5 display the account name and account type. Assign numbers for each heading, left, right, subtotal and total account before entering each account.

- Double click General Ledger Icon from the main window.

The General Ledger Window displays.

- Click **Edit**.
- Click **Create**.

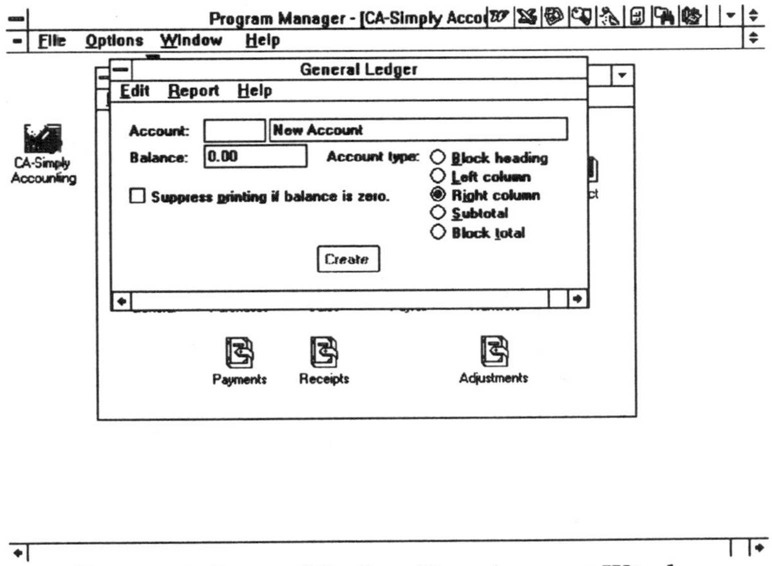


*Figure 3.3 General Ledger New Account Window*

Krystal' s Boutique
Balance Sheet
April 1, 1992

| | |
|---|---|
| ASSETS** | |
| 1000 Current Assets H | |
| Cash **R** | $15,825 |
| Petty Cash **R** | 300 |
| Accounts Receivable **R** | 14,850 |
| Interest Receivable **R** | |
| Inventory **R** | 36,180 |
| Supplies **R** | 2,240 |
| Prepaid Insurance **R** | 4,800 |
| Total Current Assets **T** | 74,195 |
| Long Term Investments **H** | |
| Notes Receivable, Long Term **R** | 13,800 |
| Total Long Term Investments **T** | 13,800 |
| Plant Assets **H** | |
| Store Equipment **L** | 18,500 |
| Acc Depre- Store Equipment **L** | -8,600 |
| Total Plant Assets **S** | 9,900 |
| Total Plant Assets T | 9,900 |
| TOTAL ASSETS ** | 97,895 |
| LIABILITIES** | |
| Current Liabilities **H** | |
| Accounts Payable **R** | 9,750 |
| Salary Payable **R** | 725 |
| Interest Payable **R** | 0 |
| Unearned Sales Revenue **R** | 3,800 |
| Notes Payable, Short Term **R** | 00000 |
| Total Current Liabilities **T** | 14,275 |
| Long Term Liabilities **H** | |
| Notes Payable, Long Term **R** | 38,800 |
| Total Long Term Liabilities T | 38,800 |
| Total Liabilities** | 53,075 |
| EQUITY** | |
| Stockholders' Equity H | |
| Common Stock **R** | 1,000 |
| Retained Earnings R | 43,820 |
| Current Earnings **X** (account exists) | 0 |
| Total Stockholders' Equity T | 44,820 |
| TOTAL EQUITY** | 44,820 |
| LIABILITIES AND EQUITY** | 97,895 |

**Headings established by CA-Simply Accounting program.

*Figure 3.4 Krystal's Boutique Balance Sheet*

| Krystal's Boutique<br>Income Statement<br>April 1, 1992 | |
|---|---|
| REVENUE** | |
| Revenue H | |
| Sales Revenue L | $0 |
| Sales Discounts L | 0 |
| Sales Returns and Allowances L | 0 |
| Net Sales S | 0 |
| Service Revenue **R** | 0 |
| Interest Revenue **R** | 0 |
| Total Revenue T | 0 |
| | |
| TOTAL REVENUE** | 0 |
| EXPENSE** | |
| | |
| Cost of Goods Sold H | |
| Purchases L | 0 |
| Purchase Discounts L | 0 |
| Purchase Returns and Allowances L | 0 |
| Net Purchases S | 0 |
| Total Cost of Goods Sold T | 0 |
| | |
| Expense H | |
| Salary Expense **R** | 0 |
| Rent Expense **R** | 0 |
| Advertising Expense **R** | 0 |
| Depreciation Expense **R** | 0 |
| Utilities Expense **R** | 0 |
| Supplies Expense **R** | 0 |
| Interest Expense **R** | 0 |
| Insurance Expense R | 0 |
| Total Expenses T | 0 |
| | |
| TOTAL EXPENSES** | 0 |
| | |
| NET INCOME** | $0 |

**Headings established by CA-Simply Accounting program.

*Figure 3.5 Krystal's Boutique Income Statement*

*Note: The 3600 Current Earnings Account is already entered. You cannot use account number 3600.*

- Enter the account number **1000**.
- Press the **TAB** Key.
- Enter **Current Assets**.
- Press the **TAB** Key.
- Click the **Block Heading** button or **TAB** to Block Heading.

The General Ledger Window with the new account Current Assets displays.

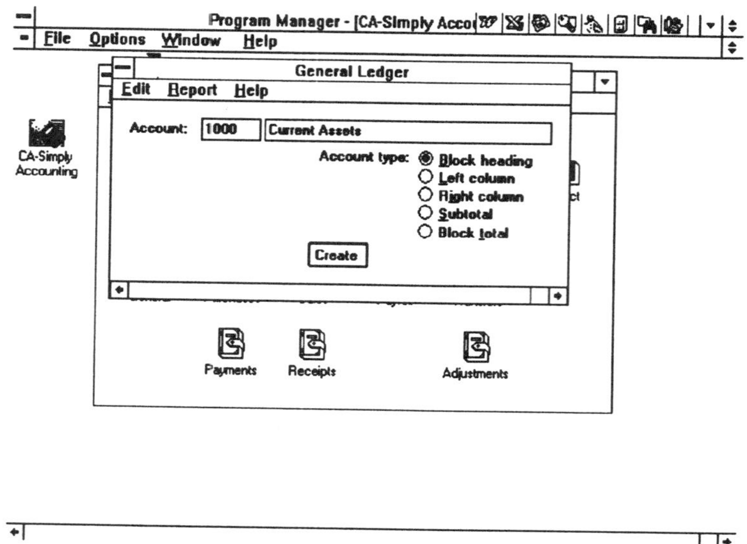


*Figure 3.6 New Account Window Completed*

- Click **Create**.

Enter the remaining accounts, entering the beginning balances if given. Remember to enter negative amounts for contra accounts. For example to enter Accum. Depre- Store Equipment:

- Enter the **account number**.
- Press the **TAB** key.
- Enter **-8,600**.
- Press the **TAB** key.
- Click **L** for Left Column.
- Click **Create**.

After entering all accounts from the balance sheet and income statement, print the chart of accounts.

## Edit Chart of Accounts

To review or edit the accounts, from the general ledger window:

- Click **Edit**.
- Click **Find**.

The list of accounts displays.

- Select the account to edit.
- Enter any changes and close the general ledger window.

## Print Chart of Accounts

**To print the chart of accounts:**

- Click **Report** from the General Ledger window or **Click General** then select **Report** from the menu bar.
- Click **Display Chart of Accounts**.

The chart of accounts displays on the screen.

- Click **File**.
- Click **Print**.
- Close the chart of accounts window.
- Close the accounts window to return to the main window.

## Printing the Trial Balance

The trial balance will display all accounts with balances, and will ensure that the debits equal the credits.

**To print the trial balance:**

- Click **Reports** from the main window.
- Click **Trial Balance**.
- Enter the period ending date.
- Click **File**.
- Click **Print**.
- Close the trial balance window.

## Backing Up Data Files

Backup of data files is a very important step in the computerized accounting system. In the computerized system, when you post your transactions, the financial statements are automatically updated. To save any activity prior to posting or after posting, you can do a backup of your data files. Another use for the backup of data files would be to allow you to go back to a previous session's work, if necessary. You can copy your backup files to your working disk, and make any changes. Keep in mind, when this is done, you will lose any work done prior to this session. The restoring of backup files will replace the existing files. When to do backups will be indicated in the practice sets.

**Making A Backup Copy**

Use File Manager to make a copy of the data disk. Keep two disks to ensure backup of your data files. From the Program Manager:

- Click **Main**.
- Click **File Manager**.
- Click **Disk** from the menu.
- Click **Copy Disk**.
- Place the data disk in the disk drive as your source disk.

Follow the instructions on the screen to prompt you for the destination disk.

- Replace the source disk with destination disk.
- Click **OK**.

When the copy is made, close the file manager window. Label the disks appropriately.

## Setting the Module to Ready

Before transactions can be entered in the general journal, the General Module must be set to READY mode. The first step is to set the integration accounts and then set the module to Ready.
To Set the Integration Accounts:

- Single click the General Ledger Icon
- Click **Setup** from the menu bar.
- Click **General Integration Accounts**.

The general integration accounts dialog box displays.

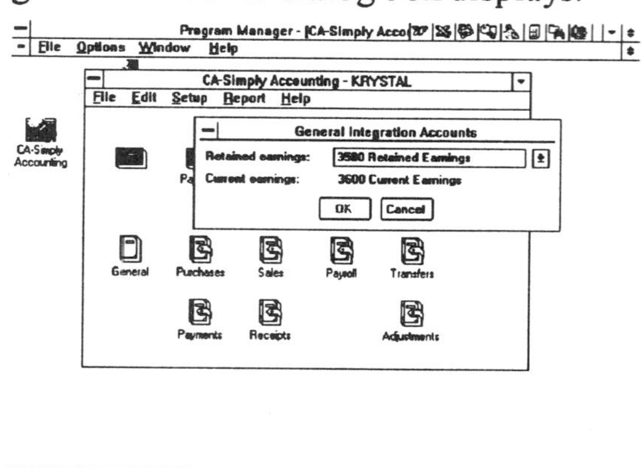


*Figure 3.7 General Integration Accounts*

- Select the **Retained Earnings Account** from the drop down list box.
- Click **OK**.

**To Set the general ledger Module to Ready:**

- Click **Setup** from the menu bar.
- Click **Set General Ready**.

You will be warned that you cannot reverse this process. If you have backed up your data files prior to this, you will be able to reverse this process.

- Click **Proceed.**

The general ledger module is in **READY** mode and now monthly transactions can be recorded.

## Exiting CA-Simply

At any time during the CA-Simply session, you can exit the program.

**To Exit CA-Simply:**

Click the **Control** menu bar in the upper left corner OR
Click **File**, then Click **Exit**.

## Chapter Summary

After completing this chapter, you have established the chart of accounts with the initial balances, printed the chart and trial balance. You can, at any time, add new accounts and balances as well. Use this chapter as, reference to set up any new companies. In Chapter 4, you will enter general ledger transactions for Krystal's Boutique.

# Chapter 4

## General Ledger

### Overview

Using an integrated accounting package allows you to enter the company transaction in the respective module. For example, if a customer purchases inventory on credit, it is clearly an accounts receivable transaction. However, cash sales, monthly rent, and other transactions that do not correspond to the function of the module, need to be recorded in the general ledger module. In this chapter, you will record the following transactions in the general ledger module.

### Objectives

1. Enter the monthly transactions in the General Ledger.
2. Print the General Journal and General Ledger.
3. Print the Trial Balance.
4. Print the Financial Statements.
5. Exit CA-Simply.

### Entering the Monthly Transactions in the General Ledger

Simply Accounting - Using Date dialog box displays. The Using Date is the date the program uses as the posting date for all journal entries made during the current session, unless you enter a different date with individual entries. To begin the session:

- Enter **04/30/92** for the Using Date.
- Click **OK**.

### Journalizing Transactions

Now that you've examined the trial balance, you are ready to journalize the following transactions for the month of April. To save time in entering transactions, record the transactions manually first.

**To Access the General Journal:**

- Double click the General Journal Icon OR Click **File** then click **Open Journal**.

The journal screen displays.

To Enter the first transaction:
Apr. 1 Paid rent $650.00, check # 125 for April.
Record the first entry using CA-Simply General Journal:

- Enter **GJ1** in the Source Field.
- Press **TAB** key to move to the Date field.
- Enter **04/01/92** and press **TAB** key.
- Enter the description of the transaction:

  **Paid rent for April.**
- Press **TAB** key.
- Press < **enter** > and the Select Account dialog box displays.
- Select **Rent Expense**.
- Enter **650.00** and press **TAB** key.
- Press < **enter** > .
- Select **Cash.**
- Press **TAB** key.
- Enter **650.00** in the Credit column.
- Click the **POST** command button.

After posting the transaction, continue entering the remaining transactions.

| | | |
|---|---|---|
| Apr. | 1 | Purchased inventory for cash. List price was $800.00 less trade discount of $175.00 from Mill Tops. |
| | 3 | Issued check # 126 to pay salaries of $1625.00, which includes Salary Payable of $725.00 from March 31. |
| | 4 | Collected interest revenue of $1300.00, check # 901. |
| | 6 | Record Cash Sales for week, $3,550.10. |
| | 8 | Paid advertising invoice, check # 127, for $30.00. |
| | 10 | Issued check # 128 to pay salaries $1625.00. |
| | 11 | Borrowed $10,000.00 from City Bank to finance operations. Krystal signed a 90-day note payable to the bank in the name of Krystal's Boutique. |
| | 11 | Purchased inventory for cash, $625.43. |
| | 12 | Paid utilities $450.00, check # 129. |
| | 13 | Record Cash Sales of $3,010.60 for the week. |
| | 17 | Issued check # 130 to pay salaries, $1625.00. |
| | 19 | Record Cash Sales for week, $3,863.99. |
| | 22 | Received interest check for $109.59, check # 202. |

22 Performed alterations on suit and received $45.00, check # 210.
24 Issued check # 131 to pay salaries, $1625.00.
27 Record Cash Sales for week, $3,948.36.
30 Paid loan payment (Long Term Note)to Laurel Bank for $1,288.00, check# 132, including $210.00 in interest.
30 Record Cash Sales for week, $3,797.80.

CA-Simply posts each entry as it is completed. If an entry is entered incorrectly and you have posted the entry, you may correct the posted entry by entering the correct entry.

## Printing the Financial Statements

Once all adjusting entries are recorded and posted, you should print the trial balance and the financial reports.
Printing Reports
When all entries have been entered, Click **Report** from the menu bar and select the report to print. The reports to print are

- General Journal
- Trial Balance
- General Ledger

To print:

- Click on each Report name.
- Enter the date of the report, usually month end.
- Click **File**.
- Click **Print** to send to the printer.
- Close the Report window.

## Backing Up Data Files

Backup of data files is a very important step in the computerized accounting system. In the computerized system, when you post your transactions, the financial statements are automatically updated. To save any activity prior to posting or after posting, you can do a backup of your data files. Another use for the backup of data files would be to allow you to go back to a previous session's work, if necessary. You can copy your backup files to your working disk, and make any changes. Keep in mind that, when this is done, you will lose any work done prior to this session. The restoring of backup files will replace the existing files. When to do backups will be indicated in the practice sets.

**Making A Backup Copy**

Use File Manager to make a copy of the data disk. Keep two disks to ensure backup of your data files. From the Program Manager:

- Click **Main**.
- Click **File Manager**.
- Click **Disk** from the menu.
- Click **Copy Disk**.
- Place the data disk in the disk drive as your source disk.

Follow the instructions on the screen to prompt you for the destination disk.

- Replace the source disk with destination disk.
- Click **OK**.

When the copy is made, close file manager window. Label the disks appropriately.

## Exiting CA-Simply

After completing the transactions and printing all reports, you should exit CA-Simply.

**To Exit CA-Simply:**

Click the **Control** menu bar in the upper left corner OR
Click **File**, then Click **Exit**.

## Chapter Summary

In this chapter, you have completed the accounting cycle, enter transactions in the general ledger, print financial reports, and back up the data files for Krystal's Boutique. Chapter 5 will work with the Accounts Receivable module.

# Chapter 5

## Accounts Receivable

### Overview

In this chapter, you will work with the Accounts Receivable module. To computerize Krystal's accounts, you need to add the customer list, enter beginning balances and enter the integration accounts to link the transactions to the general ledger. After the setup is complete, you will process invoices and payments for the month of April.

### Objectives

After completing this chapter, you will be able:

1. Initialize Accounts Receivable module.
2. Enter invoices and payments for the current period.
3. Print Accounts Receivable reports.
4. Backup the data files.
5. Exit CA-Simply.

### Initializing the Accounts Receivable Module

When converting from a manual system to a computerized system, there are necessary housekeeping activities to perform. In order to set up customer files and all integration accounts, data files need to be created. Enter CA-Simply and select **KRYSTAL**. The necessary steps to set up an accounts receivable module are:

1. Establish the Customer accounts.
2. Enter historical data.
3. Print Accounts Receivable reports.
4. Setup Integration Accounts.
5. Set Accounts Receivable to Ready.
6. Backup data files.
7. Exit CA-Simply.

Entering data in the accounts receivable module reduces redundancy in the accounting books. You will be able to enter the transactions directly into the customer accounts and the transaction will be posted to the customer account (subsidiary ledger) as well as the accounts receivable account (parent) in the general ledger.

## Establish the Customer Accounts

The customer account information must be entered in order to process any invoices or payments. To begin,

- Click the Receivables Ledger Icon from the main window.

The new customer dialog box displays.

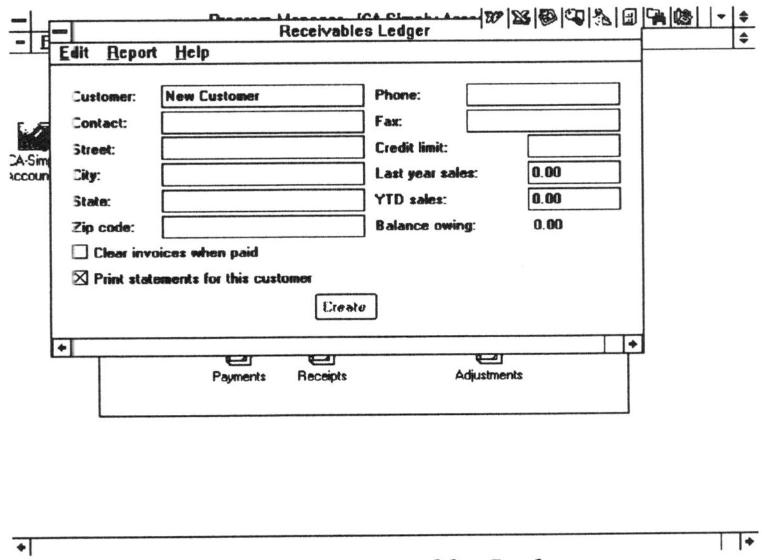


*Figure 5.1 Receivables Ledger*

- Enter **Nick Calmon**.
- Press the **TAB** key twice.
- Enter **10 Sand Street**.
- Press the **TAB** key.
- Enter **Beverly Hills**.
- Press the **TAB** key.
- Enter **CA**.
- Press the **TAB** key.
- Enter **90210**.

The completed customer screen displays.

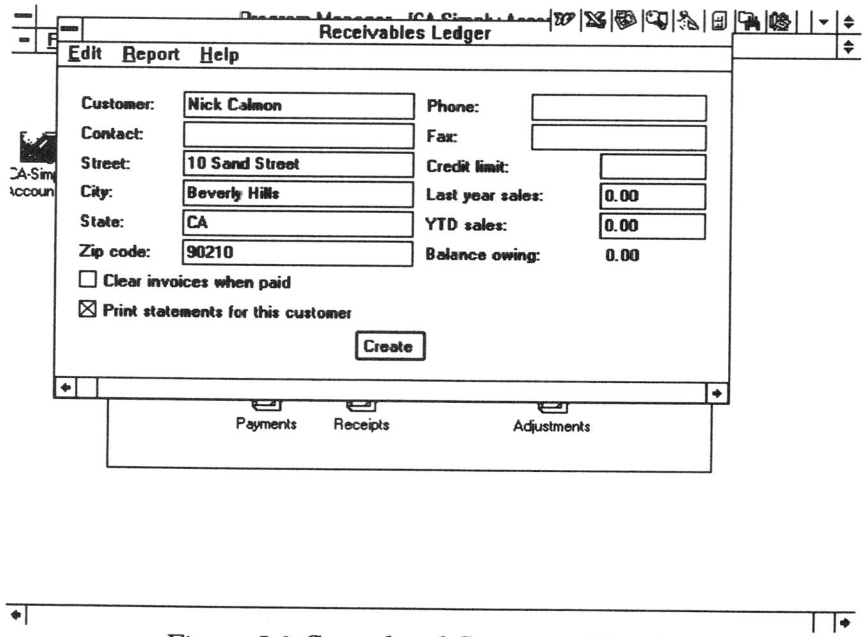


*Figure 5.2 Completed Customer Window*

- Click **Create**.

Continue entering the remaining customers.

S. Smalley
P.O. Box 10
Beverly Hills, CA 90210

Clayton Fields
1256 Cole Strip
Beverly Hills, CA 90210

Jackie Kline
4B Calvin Lane
Beverly Hills, CA 90210

Jennifer Blake
1256 Boston Road
Beverly Hills, CA 90210

Sean Duncan
River Road
Beverly Hills, CA 90210

W.D. Swift
Times Rue
Beverly Hills, CA 90210

TR Customs
62 Flame Road
Beverly Hills, CA 90210

James Finley
P.O. Box 151
Beverly Hills, CA 90210

On March 31, 1992, the amount of accounts receivable was $14,850 from the following customers:

| | | |
|---|---|---|
| **Nick Calmon** | | |
| March 15 | Invoice # 295 | $2,400.00 |
| **S. Smalley** | | |
| March 22 | Invoice # 290 | 3,850.00 |
| **Sean Duncan** | | |
| March 29 | Invoice # 292 | 925.00 |
| **Clayton Fields** | | |
| March 25 | Invoice # 291 | $1,000.00 |
| **W.D. Swift** | | |
| March 31 | Invoice # 297 | 3,500.00 |
| **Jackie Kline** | | |
| March 31 | Invoice # 299 | 400.00 |
| **TR Customs** | | |
| March 24 | Invoice # 289 | 2,075.00 |
| **Jennifer Blake** | | |
| March 27 | Invoice # 296 | 700.00 |

**Entering Historical Data**

All prior month invoices must be entered as historical data.

- Double click Receivables Ledger Icon.
- Click **Edit**.
- Click **Find**.
- Select the customer.
- Click **Invoice**.
- Enter the Invoice number.
- Enter the Invoice date.
- Enter the Invoice amount.
- Click **Record**.
- Click **Done**.

**Print Reports**

From the Report menu on the main window, print each of the following reports:

- Customer List
- Customer Aged

## Backing Up Data Files

Backup of data files is a very important step in the computerized accounting system. In the computerized system, when you post your transactions, the financial statements are automatically updated. To save any activity prior to posting or after posting, you can do a backup of your data files. Another use for the backup of data files would be to allow you to go back to a previous session's work, if necessary. You can copy your backup files to your working disk, and make any changes. Keep in mind that, when this is done, you will lose any work done prior to this session. The restoring of backup files will replace the existing files. When to do backups will be indicated in the practice sets.

**Making A Backup Copy**

Use File Manager to make a copy of the data disk. Keep two disks to ensure backup of your data files. From the Program Manager:

- Click **Main**.
- Click **File Manager**.
- Click **Disk** from the menu.
- Click **Copy Disk**.
- Place the data disk in the disk drive as your source disk.

Follow the instructions on the screen to prompt you for the destination disk.

- Replace the source disk with destination disk.
- Click **OK**.

When the copy is made close file manager window. Label the disks appropriately.

## Setting the Module to Ready

Before transactions can be entered in the sales journal and the receipts journal, the Accounts Receivable module must be set to READY mode. The first step is to set the integration accounts and then set the module to READY.
To Set the Integration Accounts

- Click **Setup** from the menu bar.
- Click **Receivables Integration Accounts**.

The Accounts Receivable integration accounts dialog box displays.

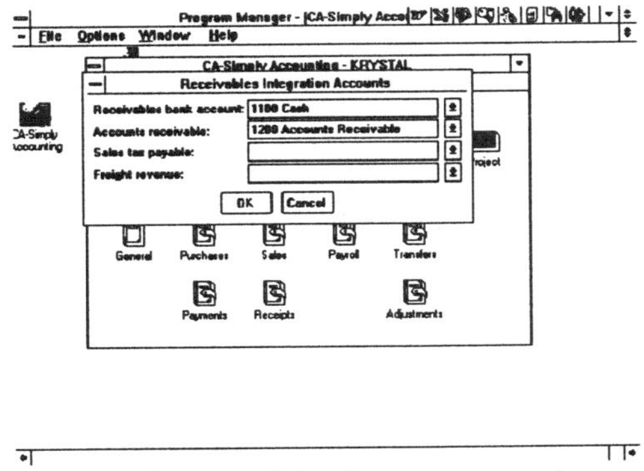

*Figure 5.3 Receivables Integration Accounts*

- Select the **Cash** account from the drop down list.
- Select the **Accounts Receivable** account from the drop down list.
- Click **OK**.

**To Set the Accounts Receivable Module to Ready**

- Click Receivables Ledger Icon.
- Click **Setup** from the menu bar.
- Click **Set Receivable Ready**.

You will be warned that you cannot reverse this process. If you have backed up your data files prior to this, you will be able to reverse this process.

- Click **Proceed.**.

The Accounts Receivable module is in READY mode and now monthly transactions can be recorded.

## Entering Invoices and Payments for Current Period

After setting the module to READY, you can enter the accounts receivable transactions for the month of April. Assume all customers credit terms are **2/10, n/30** unless otherwise stated. As you enter invoices and payments, you may have to add customers.

**To enter the sale on credit:**

Apr. 1 Sold inventory on credit for $325.00, issuing invoice 301, Nick Calmon.

- Double click **Sales Icon**.

The Sales Journal Displays.

- Select **Nick Calmon** from the drop down list box.

The information from the customer file appears.

- Click the Invoice box and enter **301**.
- Click the Date box.
- Enter **04/01/92**.
- Click the Description column and enter **Inventory**.
- Press the **TAB** key to move to the amount column.
- Enter **325.00**.
- Press the **TAB** key.
- Press < **enter** > and the chart of accounts displays.
- Select **Sales Revenue** and press < **enter** > .

The total amount displays. Before completing the invoice, review the transaction created.

- Click **Report, Display Sales Journal Entry**.

The journal entry displays. Close the window to return to the sales journal.

- Click **Post**.

**To Record a Sales Discount:**
For all sales discounts, you will need to calculate the discount amount manually. The first step is to check the discount period, and then enter the discount amount in the Sales Journal as a negative sale.

**To enter the discount:**

- Double click **Sales Icon**.
- Select the customer.
- Enter the same invoice number, for example, 301D to represent a discount recorded.
- Enter the date of the transaction.
- Enter **Discount** in the description column.
- Enter the amount as a negative number.
- Select the Sales Discount Account number.
- Click **Post**.

**Entering a Credit Memo:**

- Double click Sales Icon.

- Select the customer.
- Enter CM and a number to designate a credit memo.
- Enter the date.
- Enter Return of inventory or specific description in the Description column.
- Enter the amount as a negative number.
- Select Sales Returns and Allowances for the account.
- Click Post.

**To Record the Payment:**

Apr. 8 Received payment for prior month balance from Nick Calmon, check # 352.

- Double click Receipts Icon.

The Receipts Journal displays.

- Select Nick Calmon from the drop down box.
- Enter the check number, 352.
- Click the Invoice# 295 and the payment amount.

If the payment amount is different from the invoice amount, enter the new amount. If a discount applies to the invoice, click the invoice with negative balance.

- Click **POST** when payment is complete.

Enter the remaining transactions for each customer for the month of April.

| | | |
|---|---|---|
| Apr. | 2 | Sold inventory on credit, $150.95, invoice # 302 to Jennifer Blake. |
| | 2 | Issued invoice # 303 for sale on account to S. Smalley, $420.75. |
| | 4 | Sold inventory on credit $235.00, invoice # 304 to Sean Duncan. |
| | 5 | Issued invoices: # 305 $118.62<br># 306 $204.35<br># 307 $ 59.25<br>for sale of inventory on account to T.R. Customs. |
| | 6 | Received $400.00, check # 444, in advance for inventory ordered but not yet shipped to Clayton Fields, invoice # 308. ***Hint: Enter as Cash Sale in the Sales Journal.*** |
| | 6 | Sold inventory on credit to W.D. Swift for $315.25, invoice # 309. |
| | 6 | Issued invoice # 310 for alterations, W.D. Swift, $22.75. |

Apr. 10 Received check # 410 from April 2 invoice# 303, S. Smalley.
***Calculate the discount.***

12 Granted a sales allowance of $45.00 to Jennifer Blake, issuing credit memo # 225.
***Hint: Enter as a credit memo.***

13 Received payment for invoices # 305 and # 307 from TR Customs, check # 2900. ***Be sure to calculate each discount separately.***

14 Received half of **beginning** balance from Sean Duncan, check # 425.

14 Issued invoice # 311 for sale on account to Nick Calmon for $375.80.

14 Issued invoice # 312 for alterations, Jackie Kline, $52.50.

14 Sold inventory on account to Clayton Fields for $225.25, issuing invoice # 313.

16 Issued credit memo # 226 issued for $33.00 to TR Customs for invoice # 306 on April 5.

17 Received $200.00 for dress on order from Jackie Kline, check # 466.

18 Issued invoices # 314 for $82.50; # 315 for$35.40; and # 316 for $125.50 to Jackie Kline, for sale of inventory.

19 Sold inventory and invoiced James Finley for $232.82, # 317.

21 Issued invoice # 318, $52.29, to Jennifer Blake for alterations done.

23 Received payment for the remainder of the beginning balance amount from Sean Duncan, check # 878.

24 Sold inventory to Nick Calmon, $215.25 invoice# 319.

25 Received payment for beginning balance from S. Smalley, check# 902.

28 Granted sales allowance to Jackie Kline, $50.00, on invoice # 316. Credit memo # 227.

## Printing Accounts Receivable Reports

After completing the transactions, print the necessary Accounts Receivable reports.

To print reports,

- Click Receivables Icon.
- Select **Report** from the menu bar.
- Select Customer Aged.

- Select **Detail**, Select **All**, Click **OK**.
- Select **File**, Select **Print**.

## Printing General Ledger Reports

To print reports,

- Click General Icon.
- Click **Reports**.
- Select **General Ledger**.
- Enter the date and click **OK**.
- Click **File**.
- Click **Print**.
- Close the report window.
- Repeat the steps for the Trial Balance, Income Statement, and Balance Sheet

## Exiting CA-Simply

After completing the transactions and printing all reports, you should backup your files and exit CA-Simply.

**To Exit CA-Simply:**

Click the **Control** menu bar in the upper left corner OR
Click **File**, then Click **Exit**.

## Chapter Summary

You have established the customer accounts and worked with the accounts receivable module. You are able to balance the customer balances to the Accounts Receivable account in the general ledger automatically. In Chapter 6, you will work with Accounts Payable module.

# Chapter 6

## Accounts Payable

### Overview

In Chapter 6, you will work with the Accounts Payable module. You will initialize the accounts payable module, enter vendor information and beginning balances, and process the month's purchases and payments. The transactions entered for each vendor will automatically post to the vendor account (subsidiary ledger) and the Accounts Payable account (parent account) in the the general ledger.

### Objectives

After completing this chapter you will be able to:

1. Enter the Vendor Information.
2. Enter Historical Balances.
3. Enter purchases and payments.
4. Print Accounts Payable reports.
5. Backup data files.
6. Exit CA-Simply.

### Initializing Accounts Payable Module

After reviewing the books, the vendors owed are listed with their balances. In order to enter the current month's transactions, certain setup procedures need to be completed. The necessary steps in the accounts payable setup are:

1 .Establish the Vendor accounts.
2. Enter Historical Data.
3. Print Reports.
4. Set the Accounts Payable module to Ready.
5. Enter Invoices and Payments.
6. Print Reports.

Entering data in the accounts payable module reduces redundancy in the accounting books. You will be able to enter the transactions directly into the vendor accounts and the transaction will be posted to the vendor account (subsidiary ledger) as well as the accounts payable account (parent) in the general ledger.

## Establish the Vendor Accounts

The vendor account information must be entered in order to process any invoices or payments. Double click the Payables Ledger Icon from the main window, to begin. The new vendor dialog box displays.

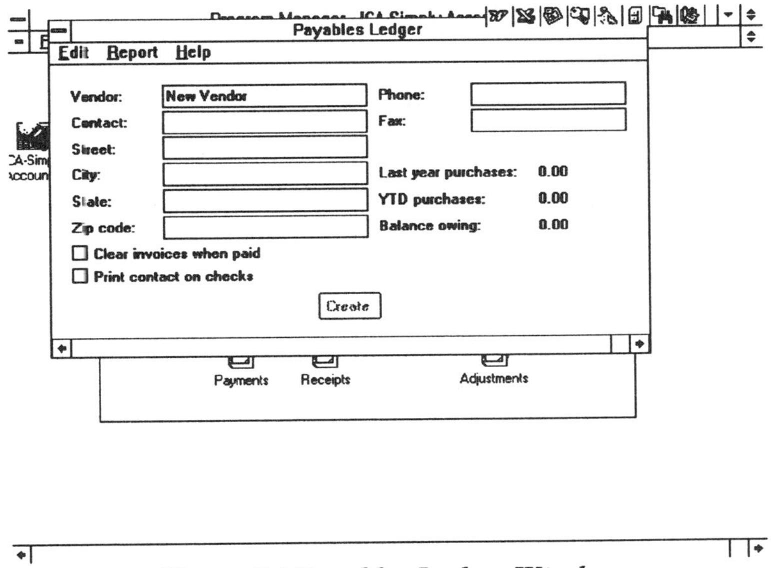


*Figure 6.1 Payables Ledger Window*

- Enter **Mill Tops**.
- Press the **TAB** key twice.
- Enter **PO Box 142**.
- Press the **TAB** key.
- Enter **Beverly Hills**.
- Press the **TAB** key.
- Enter **CA**.
- Press the **TAB** key.
- Enter **90210**.

The completed vendor screen displays.

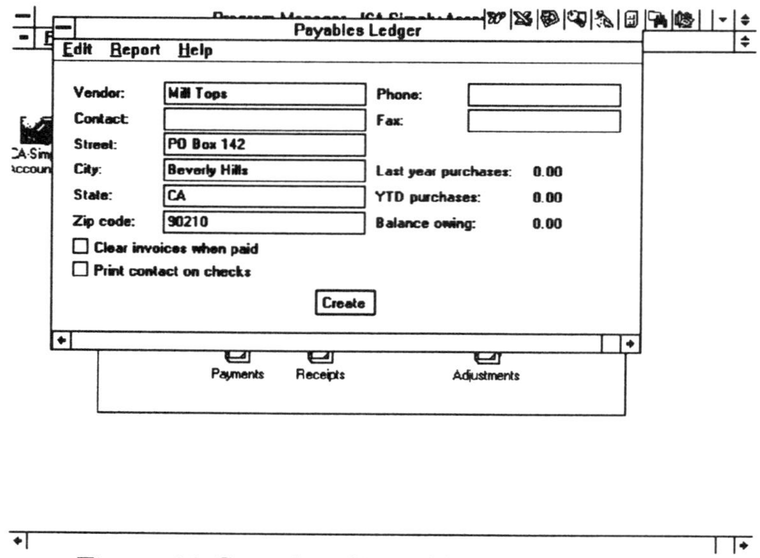


*Figure 6.2 Completed Payables Ledger Window*

- Click **Create**.

Continue entering the remaining customers.

The Accounts Payable owed on March 31, 1992 was $9,750 and was payable to the following vendors:

C.W. Palmetto
P.O. Box 456
Beverly Hills, CA 90210

E & G Stationary
River Cliff
Beverly Hills, CA 90210

Computer World
Seaside Road
Beverly Hills, CA 90210

Dockers Unlimited
P.O. Box 1678
Beverly Hills, CA 90210

Dees Collections
P.O. Box 900
Beverly Hills, CA 90210

On April 1, 1992, the amount of accounts payable was $9,750 from the following vendors:

**Mill Tops**

| March 15 | Invoice # 25 | $ 3,200.00 |
|---|---|---|

| | | |
|---|---|---|
| **C.W. Palmetto** | | |
| March 18 | Invoice# 42 | 550.00 |
| **Dockers Unlimited** | | |
| March 30 | Invoice# 6678 | 3,500.00 |
| **E & G Stationary** | | |
| March 31 | Invoice# 24900 | 750.00 |
| **Dees Collections** | | |
| March 27 | Invoice # 2567 | 1,750.00 |

**Entering Historical Data**

All prior month invoices must be entered as historical data.

- Double click the Payables Ledger Icon.
- Click **Edit**.
- Click **Find**.
- Select the vendor.
- Enter the Invoice number.
- Enter the Invoice date.
- Enter the Invoice amount.
- Click **Record**.
- Click **Done**.

**Print Reports**

From the Report menu, with the Payables Icon highlighted, print each of the following reports:

- Vendor List
- Vendor Aged

## Backing Up Data Files

Backup of data files is a very important step in the computerized accounting system. In the computerized system, when you post your transactions, the financial statements are automatically updated. To save any activity prior to posting or after posting, you can do a backup of your data files. Another use for the backup of data files would be to allow you to go back to a previous session's work, if necessary. You can copy your backup files to your working disk, and make any changes. Keep in mind that, when this is done, you will lose any work done prior to this session. The restoring of backup files will replace the existing files. When to do backups will be indicated in the practice sets.

**Making A Backup Copy**
Use File Manager to make a copy of the data disk. Keep two disks to ensure backup of your data files. From the Program Manager:

- Click **Main**.
- Click **File Manager**.
- Click **Disk** from the menu.
- Click **Copy Disk**.
- Place the data disk in the disk drive as your source disk.

Follow the instructions on the screen to prompt you for the destination disk.

- Replace the source disk with destination disk.
- Click **OK**.

When the copy is made close file manager window. Label the disks appropriately.

## Setting the Module to Ready

Before transactions can be entered in the sales journal and the receipts journal, the Accounts Payable module must be set to READY mode. The first step is to set the integration accounts and then set the module to READY.
To Set the Integration Accounts

- Click **Setup** from the menu bar.
- Click **Payable Integration Accounts**.

The Accounts Payable Integration Accounts dialog box displays.

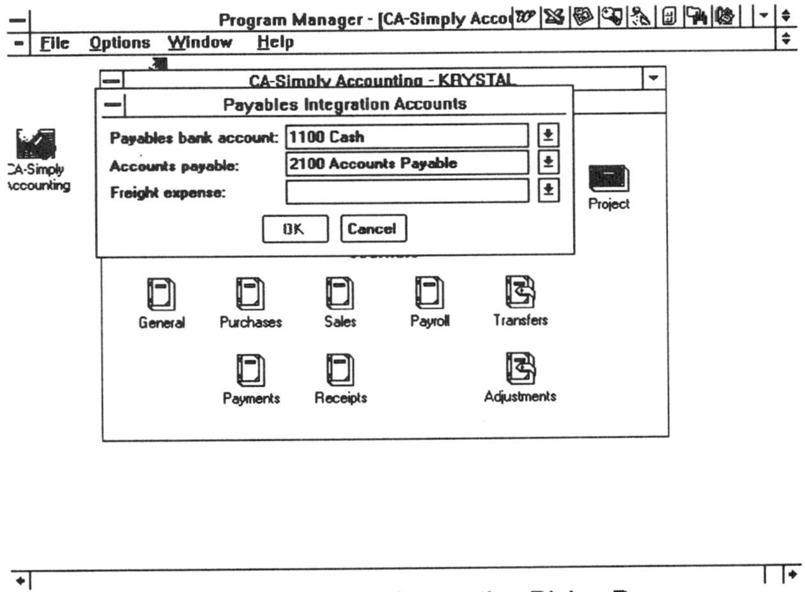


Figure 6.3 Payables Integration Dialog Box

- Select the **Cash** account from the drop down list.
- Select the **Accounts Payable** account from the drop down list.
- Click **OK**.

**To Set the Accounts Payable Module to Ready**

- Click **Setup** from the menu bar.
- Click **Set Payables to Ready**.

You will be warned that you cannot reverse this process. If you have backed up of your data files prior to this, you will be able to reverse this process.

- Click **Proceed**.

The Accounts Payable module is in READY mode and now monthly transactions can be recorded.

## Entering Invoices and Payments for Current Period

After setting the module to **READY**, you can enter the accounts receivable transactions for the month of April. As you enter invoices and payments, you may have to add customers.

**To enter the purchase on credit:**

Apr. 3 Purchased inventory on credit from Mill Tops for $1200.00, invoice# 410

- Double click **Purchases Icon**.

The Purchases Journal displays.

- Select **Mill Tops** from the drop down list box.

The information from the customer file appears.

- Click the Invoice box and enter **410**.
- Click the Date box.
- Enter **04/03/92.**
- Press the **TAB** key to move to the amount column.
- Enter **1200.00**.
- Press the **TAB** key.
- Press < **enter** > and the chart of accounts displays.
- Select **Purchases** and **press < enter >** .

The total amount displays. Before completing the invoice, review the transaction created.

- Click **Report**, **Display Purchase Journal Entry**.

The journal entry displays. Close the window to return to the sales journal.

- Click **POST**.

**To record a purchase discount:**

For all purchase discounts, you will need to calculate the discount amount manually. The first step is to check the discount period, and then enter the discount amount in the Purchases Journal as a negative amount.

To enter the discount:

- Double click **Purchases Icon**.
- Select the vendor.
- Enter the same invoice number, for example, 301D to represent a discount recorded.
- Enter the date of the transaction.
- Enter the amount as a negative number.
- Select the Purchase Discount Account number.
- Click **POST**.

**To Enter a Credit Memo:**

- Double click Purchases Icon.
- Select the customer.
- Enter **CM** and a number to designate a credit memo.
- Enter the date.
- Enter Return of inventory or specific description in the Description column.
- Enter the amount as a negative number.
- Select **Purchase Returns and Allowances** for the account.
- Click **POST**.

**To Record the Payment:**

Apr. 14 Issued check # 129 to pay Mill Tops for the March amount owed, invoice # 25.

- Double click Payments Icon.

The Payments Journal displays.

- Select **Mill Tops** from the drop down box.
- Enter the check number, 129.
- Click the Invoice# 25 and the payment amount.

If the payment amount is different from the invoice amount, enter the new amount. If a discount applies to the invoice, click the invoice with a negative balance.

- Click **Post** when the payment is complete.

Enter the remaining transactions for each customer for the month of April.

| | | |
|---|---|---|
| Apr. | 6 | Purchased inventory on credit 3/15 n/30 from Dockers Unlimited for $2300.00, invoice # 566. |
| | 8 | Returned damaged inventory to the company from whom we made the purchase on April 6 (invoice # 566) for $225.75. ***Hint: Enter a credit memo.*** |
| | 9 | Purchased supplies for $500.00 on credit, Invoice# 222 from E & G Stationery, 2/10 n/30. Charge to an asset. |
| | 12 | Returned additional damaged inventory to CW Palmetto for $300.00. Invoice# 42. |
| | 13 | Paid amount payable in full to CW Palmetto. Check # 136. |
| | 14 | Purchased computer equipment from Computer World, $6250.00 on credit, invoice # 465. ***Hint: Add Computer Equipment account and Accumulated Depreciation*** |

***Computer Equipment Account.***

14 Purchased office furniture from Computer World for $1490.00 on credit, invoice # 466. ***Hint: Add Office Furniture account and Accumulated Depreciation Office Furniture Account.***

14 Issued check# 129 to pay Mill Tops for the March amount owed, invoice # 25.

16 Purchased inventory on credit from CW Palmetto, $1350.00, 2/10 n/30, invoice # 802.

19 Paid balance owed to E & G Stationery, check# 137.

20 Received and paid advertising invoice# 25, $150.00, check# 138 to LM Marketing. ***Hint: Enter new vendor, then enter the invoice.***

21 Purchased inventory from CW Palmetto for $1650.00, 2/10 n/30, invoice # 589.

23 Paid for office furniture from Computer World, check# 139, invoice# 466.

25 Purchased supplies $500.00 from E & G Stationery, 2/10 n/30, invoice # 903. Charge to an Asset.

26 Paid amount owed on April 16 purchase to CW Palmetto, check # 140, invoice# 802.

27 Purchased inventory $500.00, Dees Collections, 2/10 n/30, invoice# 123.

29 Returned damaged merchandise $200.00, Dees Collections, against invoice# 123.

30 Paid amount owed to Computer World, Check # 141 invoice# 465.

## Printing Accounts Payable Reports

After completing the transactions, print the necessary Accounts Payable reports.

**To print reports,**

- Click Payables Ledger Icon.
- Select **Report** from the menu bar.
- Print the Vendor Aged.

## Printing General Ledger Reports

**To print reports,**

- Click General Ledger Icon.
- Click **Reports** from the menu bar.

- Print the following reports:
  General Journal
  General Ledger
  Trial Balance
  Income Statement
  Balance Sheet

## Exiting CA-Simply

After completing the transactions and printing all reports, you should backup your files and exit CA-Simply.

**To Exit CA-Simply:**

Click the **Control** menu bar in the upper left corner OR
Click **File**, then click **Exit**.

## Chapter Summary

In this chapter, you have completed the accounts payable module. You have an accurate list of the vendors owed and payments made throughout the month. To record the adjusting entries, the General Ledger module will be used in Chapter 7.

# Chapter 7

## Adjusting Entries

### Entering the Adjusting Entries

To enter the the adjusting entries using General Journal, use ADJ1, ADJ2, and so on as the Source. Be sure to add any new accounts needed for the adjustments. ***Hint: Inventory Adjustment account.***

| | |
|---|---|
| April 30 | Accrued Interest Revenue, $250.00 |
| April 30 | Prepaid insurance reflects one year payment. Record insurance expense expired for April 30. |
| April 30 | Accrued salary expense, $1300.00 |
| April 30 | Supplies on hand, $450.00 |
| April 30 | Accrued interest expense on short term note, $10,000, 90-day, 10% note. |
| April 30 | Depreciation expense, $174.00 for the computer; $25.00 for the office furniture, and $256.00 for store equipment |
| April 30 | Inventory on hand, $32,800 |

The inventory adjustment must be made to a cost of goods sold account or an inventory adjustment account before closing. For example, you can establish a new account just for the inventory adjustment in the cost of goods sold section of the income statement. The entry will be:

Inventory
COGS Adjustment Account
or

COGS Adjustment Account
Inventory

**Adjusting the Uncollectible Accounts**

The company follows a policy of adjusting its allowance for doubtful accounts at the end of each month. It uses the balance sheet method for estimating its doubtful accounts as follows:

| | |
|---|---|
| **Current** | **1%** |
| **Over 30 days** | **5%** |
| **Over 60 days** | **20%** |
| **Over 90 days** | **50%** |

*Note: Assume beginning balances are over 30 days.*

Use the aging report to calculate the total expected amount that Krystal's Boutique should set aside as an allowance for doubtful accounts. Remember, if you do not have both Allowance for Doubtful Accounts and Bad Debt Expense Account set up, you will have to add them to your chart. Record this entry in the general journal.

## Backing Up Data Files

Backup of data files is a very important step in the computerized accounting system. In the computerized system, when you post your transactions, the financial statements are automatically updated. To save any activity prior to posting or after posting, you can do a backup of your data files. Another use for the backup of data files would be to allow you to go back to a previous session's work, if necessary. You can copy your backup files to your working disk, and make any changes. Keep in mind that, when this is done, you will lose any work done prior to this session. The restoring of backup files will replace the existing files. When to do backups will be indicated in the practice sets.

**Making A Backup Copy**
Use File Manager to make a copy of the data disk. Keep two disks to ensure backup of your data files. From the Program Manager:

- Click **Main**.
- Click **File Manager**.
- Click **Disk** from the menu.
- Click **Copy Disk**.
- Place the data disk in the disk drive as your source disk.

Follow the instructions on the screen to prompt you for the destination disk.

- Replace the source disk with destination disk.
- Click **OK**.

When the copy is made close file manager window. Label the disks appropriately.

## Printing the Financial Statements

Once all adjusting entries are recorded and posted, you should print the trial balance and the financial reports.

To print reports,

- Click General Ledger Icon.
- Select **Report** from the menu bar.
- Print General Journal
  General Ledger
  Trial Balance
  Income Statement
  Balance Sheet

## Exiting CA-Simply

After completing the transactions and printing all reports, you should and exit CA-Simply.
**To Exit CA-Simply:**
Click the **Control** menu bar in the upper left corner OR
Click **File**, then click **Exit**.

## Chapter Summary

You have completed the accounting cycle for Krystal's Boutique, using the general ledger, accounts receivable and accounts payable modules. In the last practice set, you will work with a corporation and computerize the existing company using the general, inventory, accounts receivable, accounts payable and payroll modules.

# Chapter 8

## The Energy Connection Sales and Service, Inc.

### Overview

In this chapter you will work with a sales and service corporation using the General Ledger, Inventory, Accounts Payable, Accounts Receivable, and Payroll modules to convert an existing company's manual accounting records to a computerized accounting system using the CA-Simply Accounting System. This practice set can be successfully completed after covering topics on corporations in your accounting textbook.

### Objectives

After completion of this chapter, you should be able to:

1. Setup the General Ledger module.
2. Setup the Inventory module.
3. Setup the Accounts Payable module.
4. Setup the Accounts Receivable module.
5. Setup the Payroll module.
6. Backup the data files.
7. Exit CA-Simply.

The Energy Connection Sales and Service, Inc. (ECSS) is a comprehensive practice set covering the five modules using CA-Simply Accounting System.

**General Ledger**
**Inventory**
**Accounts Receivable**
**Accounts Payable**
**Payroll**

You will convert a manual system to a computerized accounting system. In Chapter 9, you will process the ECSS accounting records for a three-month period, from April through June. This will allow the student to gain a full understanding of how transactions of one month affect other month's balances. You will print the quarterly reports payroll.

ECSS is a retail promotional supplies corporation that offers both sales and service. It is a close (non-public) corporation chartered by and operating in the state of Pennsylvania. The business will be departmentalized as follows:

**Sales -- Electrical Materials**
**Sales -- Plumbing Materials**
**Service -- Electrical**
**Service -- Plumbing**

It is important to understand the activities in the business, in order to make the correct entries for each transaction. All sales and purchases on credit with discounts are available for early payment. All sales of merchandise are subject to 5% sales tax.

The fiscal year for the business is April 1, 1991 to March 31, 1992, with April 1, 1991 (conversion date) the date on which the manual accounting system was converted to the CA-Simply Accounting system. At month end, all financial statements will be generated and files will be backed up.

In this chapter, you will establish the chart of accounts, inventory items, vendors, customers and employees with all initial amounts. For your records, you will print reports of all the historical information.

## Computerizing General Ledger

Computerizing a company requires the General Ledger to be established before the other modules. The general ledger module is updated from other module information as well as transactions within the general ledger. The steps to set up the general ledger are:

1. Create the Company ID, ECSS.
2. Enter the Company Information.
3. Construct the Chart of Accounts.
4. Set the Integration Accounts.
5. Set the module to READY.
6. Print Reports.
7. Backup data files.

Enter the following information:

**The Company Name, Address, City, State, Zip**

**The Energy Connection, Inc.**
**102 Baker Road**
**Nornstown, PA 19401-3336**

## Constructing the Chart of Accounts

The financial statements for The Energy Connection, Inc. are given. When entering the chart of accounts, you will need an account number, account name, account balance and account type. Enter account type next to the account name using the designation of:

| | |
|---|---|
| **H** | **Block Heading** |
| **L** | **Left Column** |
| **R** | **Right Column** |
| **S** | **Subtotal** |
| **T** | **Block total** |

The designation of Left and Right type accounts does not equate to debit and credit. Left and right type reflect the position the account balance will print on the financial statement. If you use left type accounts, then each group must have an S type for a subtotal and a T type for total. If you use right type accounts, then each group uses a T type for total without an S type for subtotal. CA-Simply Accounting requires all balances to be entered as positive amounts unless the account reflects a contra balance. For example, Accumulated Depreciation is a contra asset and maintains a credit balance, therefore you would enter the balance as a negative. Be sure to number the accounts in the financial statements. CA-Simply Accounting uses the following numbering system:

| | |
|---|---|
| **1000-1999** | **Assets** |
| **2000-2999** | **Liabilities** |
| **3000-3999** | **Equity** |
| **4000-4999** | **Revenue** |
| **5000-5999** | **Expenses** |

## Entering the Chart of Accounts

The financial statements display the account name, account type and beginning balance. Sample Financial statements produced in the Simply Accounting program are in **Appendix A** to assist in the design of your financial statements. Assign numbers for each heading, left, right, subtotal and total account before entering each account.

- Double click General Ledger Icon from the main window.

The General Ledger Window displays.

- Enter the account number. Remember accounts number must be assigned to headings, subtotals, and totals as well.
- Press the **TAB** key.
- Enter account name.
- Press the **TAB** key.
- Click the account type button or **TAB** to account type.

The General Ledger Window with the new account Current Assets displays.

- Click **Create**.

Enter the remaining accounts, entering the beginning balances if given. Remember to enter negative amounts for contra accounts. After entering all accounts from the balance sheet and income statement, print the chart of accounts.

## Print Chart of Accounts

The chart of accounts can be printed from the General Ledger window or the main window. To print the chart of accounts:

- From the General Ledger window , click **Report** from the menu bar.
- Click **Display Chart of Accounts**.

The chart of accounts displays on the screen.

- Click **File**.
- Click **Print**.
- Close the chart of accounts window.
- Close the accounts window to return to the main window.

## Printing the Trial Balance

The trial balance will display all accounts with balances, and will ensure that the debits equal the credits.
To print the trial balance:

- Click the General Ledger Icon.
- Click **Report** from the main window.
- Click **Trial Balance**.
- Click **File**.
- Click **Print**.
- Close the Trial Balance window.

**The Energy Connection, Inc.**
**Balance Sheet**
**April 1, 1991**

| | |
|---|---|
| **ASSETS**** | |
| **Current Assets** | |
| Cash Operating | 38,874.73 |
| Cash Payroll | 0.00 |
| Petty Cash | 100.00 |
| Accounts Receivable | 12,501.35 |
| Allow for Doubtful Accts | -500.00 |
| Notes Receivable-Short Term | 3,000.00 |
| Inventory- Electrical | 4,620.00 |
| Inventory- Plumbing | 4,950.00 |
| Office Supplies | 852.00 |
| Prepaid Insurance | 2,400.00 |
| **Total Current Assets** | **66,798.08** |
| | |
| **Plant Assets** | |
| Land | 60,000.00 |
| Buildings | 150,000.00 |
| Accum Depr-Building | -30,000.00 |
| Automotive | 65,000.00 |
| Accum Depr-Automotive | -12,000.00 |
| Computer | 5,200.00 |
| Accum Depr-Computer | -800.00 |
| **Total Plant Assets** | **237,400.00** |
| **TOTAL ASSETS**** | **304,198.08** |
| **LIABILITIES**** | |
| **Current Liabilities** | |
| Accounts Payable | 5,147.00 |
| Notes Payable, Short Term | 12,000.00 |
| Fed WH Tax Payable (FIT) | 428.95 |
| FICA Payable (SSTax Deduction) | 554.65 |
| FUTA Payable | 82.25 |
| State Income Tax Payable (SIT) | 770.35 |

| | |
|---|---|
| SUTA Payable | 24.90 |
| Company Pension Plan | 5,200.00 |
| Employee Insurance Payable | 0.00 |
| Sales Tax Payable | 1,725.35 |
| Unearned Electrical Revenue | 275.00 |
| Unearned Plumbing Revenue | 200.00 |
| Notes Payable, Sarah Merritt | 52,000.00 |
| **Total Current Liabilities** | **78,408.45** |
| | |
| **STOCKHOLDERS' EQUITY**** | |
| Stockholders' Equity | |
| Common Stock | 30,000.00 |
| Retained Earnings | 195,789.63 |
| **CURRENT EARNINGS**** | 00.00 |
| **Total Stockholders' Equity** | **225,789.63** |
| **TOTAL LIABILITIES AND STOCKHOLDERS' EQUITY**** | **304,198.08** |

**The Energy Connection, Inc.**
**Income Statement**
**April 1, 1991**

| | |
|---|---|
| **REVENUE**** | |
| **Revenue** | |
| Sales-Electrical | 00.00 |
| Sales-Plumbing | 00.00 |
| Total Net Sales | 00.00 |
| Other Revenue | |
| Service-Electrical | 00.00 |
| Service-Plumbing | 00.00 |
| Interest Revenue | 00.00 |
| **Total Other Revenue** | **00.00** |
| **Total Revenue** | **00.00** |
| | |
| **Expenses**** | |
| **Cost of Goods Sold** | |
| Cost of Goods Sold- Electrical | 00.00 |
| Cost of Goods Sold- Plumbing | 00.00 |
| **Total Cost of Goods Sold** | **00.00** |
| **Operating Expenses** | |
| Wages Expense | 00.00 |
| MedTax Expense | 00.00 |
| FICA Tax Expense (SSTax Expense) | 00.00 |
| FUTA Expense | 00.00 |
| SUTA Expense | 00.00 |

| | |
|---|---|
| SDI Expense | 00.00 |
| Fuel Expense | 00.00 |
| Insurance Expense | 00.00 |
| Repair Expense | 00.00 |
| Office Supplies Expense | 00.00 |
| Telephone Expense | 00.00 |
| Utilities Expense | 00.00 |
| Advertising Expense | 00.00 |
| License Expense | 00.00 |
| Depreciation Expense | 00.00 |
| Interest Expense | 00.00 |
| Bank Charges | 00.00 |
| **Total Operating Expenses** | **00.00** |
| **Total Expenses**** | **00.00** |
| **Net Income**** | **00.00** |

## Setting the Module to Ready

Before transactions can be entered in the general journal, the General Module must be set to READY mode. The first step is to set the integration accounts and then set the module to READY.

**To Set the Integration Accounts**

- Click the General Ledger Icon.
- Click **Setup** from the menu bar.
- Click **General Integration Accounts**.

The general integration accounts dialog box displays.

- Select the **Retained Earnings Account** from the drop down list box.
- Click **OK**.

**To Set the General Module to Ready**

- Click **Setup** from the menu bar.
- Click **Set General to Ready**.
- Click **Proceed**.

## Computerizing Inventory

The perpetual inventory method will be used. CA-Simply Accounting uses the average costing method. All inventory items must be entered in the Inventory ledger to maintain a perpetual inventory system.

- Double click the Inventory Icon

The Inventory Ledger displays. For each item, enter:

| | |
|---|---|
| Item # | **2010** |
| Name of Item | **Faucet** |
| Unit | **Each** |
| Unit Price | **45.00** |
| Min. Level | **10** |
| Quantity on Hand* | **30** |
| Total Value* | **1350.00** |
| Asset Account | **Inventory-Plumbing** |
| Revenue Account | **Sales-Plumbing** |
| Expense Account | **Cost of Goods Sold-Plumbing** |

***Note: Double click to highlight field -then type amount.***

Plumbing Inventory: (Unit will always be Each)
The accounts listed below will be the same for all inventory items.

| | |
|---|---|
| Asset Account: | Inventory - Plumbing |
| Revenue Account: | Sales - Plumbing |
| Expense Account: | Cost of Goods Sold-Plumbing |

| | | | |
|---|---|---|---|
| Item # 3022 | Kohler Toilet | | |
| Price: 95.00 | Min. level: 4 | Qty on Hand: | 20 |
| Item # 6133 | Sink | | |
| Price: 85.00 | Min. level: 4 | Qty on Hand: | 20 |

Electric Inventory: (Unit will always be Each, unless otherwise stated.)
The accounts listed below will be the same for all inventory items.

| | |
|---|---|
| Asset Account: | Inventory-Electric |
| Revenue Account: | Sales-Electric |
| Expense Account: | Cost of Goods Sold-Electrical |

| | | |
|---|---|---|
| Item# 3299 | Electric Water Heater | |
| Price: 105.00 | Min. level: 2 | Qty on Hand: 10 |
| Item# 7199 | Wiring | |
| Price: 0.23 | Unit: Foot | Min. level: 5000 ft |
| | | Qty on Hand: 10,000 ft |
| Item# 2577 | Circuit Breakers | |
| Price: 3.50 | Min. level: 5 | Qty on Hand: 220 |
| Item# 4225 | Light Switches | |
| Price: 1.25 | Min. level: 10 | Qty on Hand: 400 |

**Print Reports**

From the Report menu print each of the following reports:

- Inventory List

## Setting the Module to Ready

Before transactions can be entered in the accounts receivable and accounts payable module using inventory, the Inventory Module must be set to READY mode. ***The integration accounts should be left blank.*** Set the module to READY.

### To Set the Inventory Module to Ready

- Click **Setup** from the menu bar.
- Click **Set Inventory to Ready**.

You will be warned that you cannot reverse this process. If you have backed up of your data files prior to this, you will be able to reverse this process.

- Click **Proceed.**

## Computerizing Accounts Payable

The vendors must be entered in the Accounts Payable. The steps to set up Accounts Payable are:

1. Enter the Vendor accounts.
2. Enter historical data.
3. Print Reports.
4. Set the module to READY.

## Establish the Vendor Accounts

The vendor account information must be entered in order to process any invoices or payments. To begin,

- Double click the Payables Ledger Icon from the main window.

The new vendor dialog box displays. Enter the information for each vendor. Be sure to click **CREATE** for each vendor.

Dynamic Lighting
P.O. Box 356
Lewisburg, PA 17837

Hot and Cold, Inc.
780 Temperature Avenue
Nornstown, PA 19401

Waterworks and ETC
1096 Kings Highway
Nornstown, PA 19401-7699

Uptown Hardware Supply
4689 Wood Avenue
New York, NY 10001

**Editing a Vendor**

To edit any information entered for a vendor,

- Double click the Payables Ledger Icon.
- Click Edit.
- Click **Find**.
- Select the vendor and make the changes.
- Click **Edit**.
- Click **Create** to save changes.
- Close the Vendor Ledger window.

The Accounts Payable owed on April 1, 1991 was $5,147 and was payable to the following vendors:

**Dynamic Lighting**

| | | |
|---|---|---|
| 03/15/91 | Inv.# 366 | $725.00 |

**Waterworks and ETC.**

| | | |
|---|---|---|
| 03/28/91 | Inv.# 357 | $2,500.00 |

**Hot and Cold, Inc.**

| | | |
|---|---|---|
| 03/20/91 | Inv.# 225 | $845.50 |
| 03/25/91 | Inv.# 445 | $525.70 |

**Uptown Hardware Supply**

| | | |
|---|---|---|
| 03/25/91 | Inv# 1001 | $550.80 |

**Entering Historical Data**

All prior month invoices must be entered as historical data.

- Double click the Payables Ledger Icon.
- Click **Invoices**.
- Enter the Invoice number.
- Enter the Invoice date.
- Enter the Invoice amount.
- Click **Record**.
- Click **Done**.

Enter invoices for each vendor. If an invoice is entered incorrectly, enter a payment to remove the invoice. Display the Vender Aged report to be sure balances are correct.

**Print Reports**

From the Reports menu, print each of the following reports:

- Vendor List

- Vendor Aged . ( Click Payables Icon, then **Report** from the main window)

## Setting the Module to Ready

Before transactions can be entered in the sales journal and the receipts journal, the Accounts Payable Module must be set to READY mode. The first step is to set the integration accounts and then set the module to READY.

**To Set the Integration Accounts**

- Click **Setup** from the menu bar.
- Click **Payable Integration Accounts**.

The Accounts Payable integration accounts dialog box displays.

- Select the **Cash Operating** account from the drop down list.
- Select the **Accounts Payable** account from the drop down list.
- Click **OK**.

**To Set the Accounts Payable Module to Ready**

- Click **Setup** from the menu bar.
- Click **Set Payables Ready**.

You will be warned that you cannot reverse this process. If you have backed up your data files prior to this, you will be able to reverse this process.

- Click **Proceed**.

## Computerizing Accounts Receivable

The Accounts Receivable module contains the customer accounts, including transactions and up to date balances. The steps to establish the Accounts Receivable are:

1. Enter the customer information.
2. Enter historical data.
3. Print Reports.
4. Set Accounts Receivable module to READY.

## Establish the Customer Accounts

The customer account information must be entered in order to process any invoices or payments. To begin,

- Double click the Receivables Ledger Icon from the main window.

The new customer dialog box displays. Enter the customer information. Be sure to click **CREATE** to complete each customer ledger window. Close the Customer ledger after entering all customers.

Customer Information

Sam Rewsbee
10 Louis Street
Lewisburg, PA 17837-4211

AB Pipefitters
Box 303
Nornstown, PA 19401-3422

Taylor Sampson
35 Sattle Drive
Nornstown, PA 19401-2233

Zing Electricians
10 Twig Road
Lewisburg, PA 17837-3233

Central Plumbing
P.O. Box 225
Nornstown, PA 19401-2233

The balance in the accounts receivable account is **$12,501.35**.
The prior period invoices are:

**Sam Rewsbee**

| | | |
|---|---|---|
| 03/31/91 | Invoice # 249 | 474.92 |

**AB Pipefitters**

| | | |
|---|---|---|
| 03/30/91 | Invoice # 247 | 2,155.55 |
| 03/31/91 | Invoice # 250 | 2,859.25 |

**Taylor Sampson**

| | | |
|---|---|---|
| 03/31/91 | Invoice # 255 | 129.78 |

**Zing Electricians**

| | | |
|---|---|---|
| 03/31/91 | Invoice # 260 | 3891.40 |

**Central Plumbing**

| | | |
|---|---|---|
| 03/31/91 | Invoice # 256 | 2990.45 |

**Entering Historical Data**

All prior month invoices must be entered as historical data.

- Double click the Receivables Ledger Icon.
- Click **Edit**.
- Click **Find**.
- Select the customer.
- Enter the Invoice number.
- Enter the Invoice date.
- Enter the Invoice amount.
- Click **Record**.
- Click **Done**.

If invoices are entered incorrectly, enter a payment to reverse the amount.

**Print Reports**

From the Reports menu, print each of the following reports:

- Customer List

- Customer Aged (from Main Window)

## Setting the Module to Ready

Before transactions can be entered in the sales journal and the receipts journal, the Accounts Receivable Module must be set to READY mode. The first step is to set the integration accounts and then set the module to READY.

**Enter the Setting Menu**

- Click **Setup** from the menu bar.
- Click **Settings**.
- Enter **5%**for Sales Tax Rate.
- Click **OK**.

**To Set the Integration Accounts**

- Click **Setup** from the menu bar.
- Click **Receivable Integration Accounts**.

The Accounts Receivable integration accounts dialog displays.

- Select the **Cash Operating** account from the drop down list.
- Select the **Accounts Receivable** account from the drop down list.
- Select the **Sales Tax Payable** Account.
- Click **Proceed**.

**To Set the Accounts Receivable Module to Ready**

- Click **Setup** from the menu bar.
- Click **Set Receivable to Ready**.

You will be warned that you cannot reverse this process. If you have backed up your data files prior to this, you will be able to reverse this process.

- Click **OK**.

The Accounts Receivable module is in READY mode and now monthly transactions can be recorded.

## Computerizing Payroll

Of all the modules to computerize, payroll requires very detailed information. All employee information must be entered in the payroll ledger.

**To Enter Employee Information:**

- Double click the Payroll Ledger Icon

The Payroll Ledger displays.

- Enter the employee information.
- Click **OK**.
- Click **Create**.

***Note: Use Pennsylvania for the Tax Table for all employees. Enter time and one half for overtime rate. (Ex. 10.00 per hour regular, then 15.00 per hour for overtime.)***
***Employee Information:***

**Sarah Merritt**
Boston Road
Nornstown, PA 19401-2322
Telephone: 215-233-7688
Soc. Sec. # : 040-22-5689
Date of Birth: 05/02/51
Pay Period: 52
Pay Type: Salary
Pay Per Period: 1,000
Date Hired: 02/15/89
Filing Status: Married
Fed. Allowances: 2
**Deductions: (Entered when payroll is processed)**
Medical Insurance: 175.00
Employee Pension
Misc A 185.00

**Stephen Hunter**
98 Winston Road
Nornstown, PA 19401-3422
Telephone: 215-233-6754
Soc. Sec. # : 345-56-9800
Date of Birth: 01/20/57
Pay Period: 52
Pay Type: Hourly
Rate: 13.50
Date Hire: 01/04/90
Filing Status: Married
Fed. Allowances: 0
**Deductions: (Entered when payroll is processed)**
Insurance: 75.00
Employee Pension: 50.00

Rosie Hossier
122 Clitton Road
Lewisburg, PA 17837-3422

| | |
|---|---|
| Telephone: | 215-233-5422 |
| Soc. Sec. # : | 320-66-7865 |
| Date of Birth: | 04/15/55 |
| Pay Period: | 52 |
| Pay Type: | Hourly |
| Rate: | 14.00 |
| Date Hired: | 05/20/89 |
| Filing Status: | Single |
| Fed. Allowances: | 0 |
| **Deductions:(Entered when payroll is processed)** | |
| Insurance: | 175.00 |
| Employee Pension: | 0.00 |

**To Enter Employee Historical Data:**

- Click the Payroll Icon.
- Click **Edit**.
- Click **Find**.
- Select the employee.
- Enter the amounts listed below for YTD figures.

**Sarah Merritt**

| Y-T-D figures | |
|---|---|
| Salary | 13,000.00 |
| FIT Deduction | 1,390.00 |
| SS Tax Deduction | 845.00 |
| SS Tax Expense | 845.00 |
| FUTA Expense | 36.00 |
| SIT Deduction | 520.00 |
| Medical (Insurance) | 2275.00 |
| Benefits (Pension) | 2405.00 |

**Stephen Hunter**

| Y-T-D figures | |
|---|---|
| Regular Wages | 7,020.00 |
| FIT Deduction | 1,400.00 |
| SS Tax Deduction | 465.00 |
| SS Tax Expense | 465.00 |
| FUTA Expense | 21.00 |
| SIT Deduction | 280.00 |
| Medical (Insurance) | 975.00 |
| Benefit (Pension) | 650.00 |

| | |
|---|---|
| Rosie Hossier | |
| Y-T-D figures | |
| Regular Wages | 6,370.00 |
| FIT Deduction | 1,175.00 |
| SS Tax Deduction | 414.00 |
| SS Tax Expense | 414.00 |
| FUTA Expense | 42.00 |
| SIT Deduction | 255.00 |
| Medical (Insurance) | 975.00 |
| Benefits (Pension) | 00.00 |

**Print Reports**

From the Reports menu, print each of the following reports:

- Employee List.
- Employee...(From Main Window)

## Setting the Module to Ready

Before transactions can be entered in the sales journal and the receipts journal, the Payroll Module must be set to READY mode. The first step is to set the integration accounts and then set the module to READY.

**Enter the Setup Menu**

- Click **Settings**.
- Click **Payroll**.
- Enter the Tax Rates for SDI (.03), SUTA (.04), FUTA (.008).
- Click **OK**.

**To Set the Integration Accounts**

- Click **Setup** from the menu bar.
- Click **Payroll Integration Accounts**.

The Payroll integration accounts dialog displays.

- Enter the integration accounts using the drop down box. ***Leave Union, Local, Dental, SDI, and Advanced Rec. blank.***
- Click **OK**.

**To Set the Payroll Module to Ready**

- Click **Setup** from the menu bar.
- Click **Set Payroll Ready**.

You will be warned that you cannot reverse this process. If you have backed up your data files prior to this, you will be able to reverse this process.

- Click **Proceed.**

The Payroll module is in READY mode and now weekly transactions can be recorded.

## Backing Up Data Files

Backup of data files is a very important step in the computerized accounting system. In the computerized system, when you post your transactions, the financial statements are automatically updated. To save any activity prior to posting or after posting, you can do a backup of your data files. Another use for the backup of data files would be to allow you to go back to a previous session's work, if necessary. You can copy your backup files to your working disk, and make any changes. Keep in mind that, when this is done, you will lose any work done prior to this session. The restoring of backup files will replace the existing files. When to do backups will be indicated in the practice sets.

### Making A Backup Copy

Use File Manager to make a copy of the data disk. Keep two disks to ensure backup of your data files. From the Program Manager:

- Click **Main**.
- Click **File Manager**.
- Click **Disk** from the menu.
- Click **Copy Disk**.
- Place the data disk in the disk drive as your source disk.

Follow the instructions on the screen to prompt you for the destination disk.

- Replace the source disk with destination disk.
- Click **OK**.

When the copy is made close file manager window. Label the disks appropriately.

## Printing the Financial Statements

Once all adjusting entries are recorded and posted, you should print the trial balance and the financial reports.
To print reports,

- Select **Report** from the menu bar.
- Print General Journal<br>Trial Balance<br>Balance Sheet

## Exiting CA-Simply

After completing the transactions and printing all reports, you should and exit CA-Simply.

**To Exit CA-Simply:**

Click the **Control** menu bar in the upper left corner OR
Click File, then Click **Exit**.

## Chapter Summary

After completing this chapter, all necessary files are set up to begin processing the three months of transaction. Refer to chapters 4 through 7 to process General Ledger, Accounts Receivable and Accounts Payable transactions. Chapter 9 will include instructions to process payroll, as well as the three months of transactions.

# Chapter 9

## ECSS Inc.
## Business Activity

### Overview

In this chapter, you will work with the daily transactions of ECSS, Inc. You will record the transactions in the appropriate modules for the last quarter of the fiscal year. You will close each month and then perform the year-end process.

### Objectives

After completion of this chapter, you will be able to:

1. Select the specific module for each transaction.
2. Process the Payroll.
3. Record the Transactions for the month of April.
4. Analyze April's financial statements.
5. Record the Transactions for the month of May.
6. Record the Transactions for the month of June.

### Analyzing the Company Records

The monthly transactions should be recorded in the appropriate module. For each module, you must print reports, and backup data files. CA-Simply accounting automatically moves to the next month by the Using Date. All entries from the other modules are automatically posted to the general ledger.

You are ready to enter transactions in the appropriate module. First, you must analyze the transaction and determine the correct module to use. Questions to ask yourself when reading each transaction:

- What accounts does the transaction affect?
- Does it directly affect GL, AR, AP, or payroll?

As you prepare the entries, be aware of any accounts, vendors, customers, or employees that need to be added to the system. To enter new vendors and customers, use the name given and fill in an address, city, state and zip code. ***Hint: For discount terms in accounts receivable use 2/10, n/30. Use 40 hours as the standard work week for salary employees.***

## Processing Payroll

**The steps to process each payroll are:**

- Double click **Payroll Journal Icon**.

The Payroll Journal displays.

- Fill in the Fields required:
- Select Employee.
- Accept Check number.
- Enter Date.
- Period Start.
- Period End.
- Enter Regular Hours.
- Enter Benefits.
- Enter Medical Insurance.

The rest of the fields will fill with the amounts set up in the employee ledger.

- Click **File**.
- Click **Print** to print check.
- Click **Post**.
- Print Payroll Reports.

## Recording the Transactions for the Month of April

Apr. 1 Sold electric water heater, $225.00, and provided 3 hours electrical labor ($50.00/hr), issuing invoice to Taylor Sampson, invoice # 401.

***Note for all labor entries:***
Enter electrical or plumbing labor on invoice leaving the item field blank, entering number of hours, Hr for unit, labor as description, price as 50.00 and the account number for Service-Plumbing. **Do not charge sales tax for labor.**

Example for invoice:

- Double click Sales Icon. ( Use the Tab key to move to each field.)
- Select the customer from the drop down list box.
- Enter Invoice number.
- Enter date.
- Press **TAB**.
- Press < **enter** > in the Item field.
- Select "Electric Water Heater"
- Enter 1 for quantity.
- Enter **sales price**.
- Click **POST**.

Apr. 2 Sold faucet on credit $125.00, and provided 2 hours plumbing labor on Inv. # 402, to Sam Rewsbee.

2 Issued Inv.# 403 for sale of 1,000 feet ($0.75/ ft) of wiring; 10 light switches ($3.75 ea), 4 circuit breakers ($7.95 each) on account to Zing Electricians.

3 Purchased 8,500 feet of wiring ($0.23/ ft) on credit terms, 3/15, n/30, from Dynamic Lighting, Inv.# 224.
***Hint: Use same instruction for purchase as invoice, except click Purchase Icon.***

3 Paid telephone $84.15 to the Penn Phone Company Ck# 551.

3 Received payments from:

| | | |
|---|---|---|
| Sam Rewsbee | Inv# 290 | Ck# 441 |
| Taylor Sampson | Inv# 301 | Ck# 1025 |
| AB Pipefitters | Inv# 250 | Ck# 221 |

***Hint: Refer to chapter 5 on entering discounts.***

4 Paid IRS withholding tax $428.95, Ck# 552.

5 Purchased plumbing inventory from Hot and Cold, Inc. Inv.# 210 consisting of:

| | |
|---|---|
| 10 faucets @ $45.00 | 4 sinks @ $85.00 |
| 4 toilets @ 95.00 | 2 electric water heaters @ 105.00 |

| | |
|---|---|
| 7 | Merchandise returned for 200 feet* of wiring ($0.23)to Dynamic Lighting, Inv# 224 dated April 3. Refer to debit memo in chapter 6.<br>***Note:** Enter quantity of wire return as -200 ft (negative amount) or the inventory will be increased by 200 ft while the dollar amount is decreased. |
| 10 | Issued weekly payroll for the following employees: Pay period 04/01/91- 04/07/91. ***(Enter Medical and Benefits amounts for future pay periods.)***<br><br>**Note:** If necessary to enter a payroll entry, advance the using date from the main window, click Setup and click Advance Using Date. |

| | |
|---|---|
| Sarah Merritt | Salary |
| Benefits | 185.00 |
| Medical | 175.00 |
| Stephen Hunter | 37.5 hours |
| Benefits | 50.00 |
| Medical | 75.00 |
| Rosie Hossier | 20 hours |
| Medical | 75.00 |

| | |
|---|---|
| 10 | Record bank transfer from Cash Operating to Cash Payroll. Display the trial balance for payroll date and transfer the amount needed to maintain a zero balance in the Cash Payroll account. |
| 10 | Received payment of Inv# 401 dated April 1 from Taylor Sampson, Ck.# 342. Refer to chapter 5 on entering discounts. |
| 13 | Paid Inv# 224 dated April 3 to Dynamic Lighting, Ck.# 553. |
| 15 | Paid telephone bill, Sprint, $45.15 Ck.# 554. |
| 15 | Paid gasoline bill to Mobil Oil, $65.50 Ck.# 555. |
| 16 | Issued Inv# 404 for plumbing inventory and labor to Central Plumbing, consisting of:<br>1 toilet for $195.00 — 1 sink for $190.00<br>1 faucet for $125.00 — Labor (8 hours @ $50.00) |

16 Received a Notes Receivable for $2,000 for 1 month at 8% from Central Plumbing, check # 556.

17 Issued weekly payroll. Remember the benefits and medical amounts,
Pay period:04/08/91 - 04/14/91

| | |
|---|---|
| Sarah Merritt | Salary |
| Stephen Hunter | 37.5 hours |
| Rosie Hossier | 35 hours |

17 Record bank transfer from Cash Operating to Cash Payroll.

18 Collected interest revenue from note receivable of $30.00, Ck# 224.

20 Paid state sales tax for March, Ck.# 557.

24 Issued weekly payroll. ***(Remember Medical and Benefit amounts.)***
Pay period: 04/15/91 - 04/21/91

| | |
|---|---|
| Sarah Merritt | Salary |
| Stephen Hunter | 30.5 hours |
| Rosie Hossier | 30 hours |

24 Record bank transfer from Cash Operating to Cash Payroll.

25 Issued Inv.# 405 to:
Zing Electricians 1,000 feet of wiring ($0.75/ft), 4 breakers ($7.95 ea) and 2 light switches ($3.75 ea).

26 Received $400.00, in advance, for electrical job (labor) ordered but not performed from Sam Rewsbee. Charge to unearned account, Inv. # 406, Ck. # 810.

26 Purchased electrical inventory on credit 2/15 n/30 from Uptown Hardware Supply for $315.00, Inv.# 5777, consisting of 3 electric water heaters.

26 Sold plumbing inventory on credit to Taylor Sampson for $195.00, 1 toilet and provided 4 hours installation labor, Inv.# 407.

27 Returned damaged plumbing inventory to the company we purchased it from April 5, Inv. # 210 for 2 sinks ($85.00 each). Enter quantity as -2 sinks (negative quantity).

27 Received and paid advertising invoice for $30.00 to The Day Paper, Ck.# 558.

28 Received payment for Inv.# 407 from Taylor Sampson, Ck. # 73.

29 Purchased office supplies for $500.00 from City Stationery, 2/10 n/30. Set up new account. Inv. # 112. (New vendor address: 80 Water Ave. Nornstown, PA.)

29 Add another item to inventory:
Electric Utility Box, Item# 2750, Cost $2.25, Minimum 10 each.

29 Purchased 20 electric utility boxes from Dynamic Lighting ($2.25 ea), Inv.# 2562.

30 Borrowed $15,000 from City Bank. Merritt signed a 10% 60 - day note payable to the bank in the name of The Energy Connection, Inc.

30 Recorded log book for service calls for month of April: Assign Invoice numbers to each.
***Note: Journal Date will be 4/30. Enter service date and work description in the comments column.***

Invoices prepared for:

Taylor Samson
4/4 Inv. # 408 — Repaired dishwasher
Electrical Labor 2 Hours

John and Sue Tolland (new customer)
4/6 Inv. # 409 — Heating System Repaired
1 Electric Water Heater $225.00
Plumbing Labor 4 hours

Sam Rewsbee
4/10 Inv. # 410 — Replaced bathroom faucet
1 faucet, $125.00
Plumbing Labor 2 Hours

AB Pipefitters

| | |
|---|---|
| 4/18 Inv. # 411 | Installation of water heater<br>1 electric water heater $225.00<br>Plumbing Labor 3 Hours |

**Preparing Adjusting Entries**

Once the trial balance has been printed, make the following adjusting entries. Use ADJ as the posting reference.

| | | |
|---|---|---|
| April | 30 | Accrued interest revenue, $41.50 |
| April | 30 | Supplies on hand, $450.00 |
| April | 30 | Prepaid insurance expired, $650.00 |
| April | 30 | Accrued Interest expense, $125.00 |
| April | 30 | Depreciation expense, $200.00 for the computer; $250.00 for automotive, and $1,000 for building. |
| April | 30 | Balance of Unearned electrical revenue, $400.00 |

Enter the following transaction to replenish petty cash:

| | | | |
|---|---|---|---|
| Apr. | 15 | Coffee supplies | 22.75 |
| | 18 | Computer ribbons | 15.00 |
| | 20 | Gas for company car | 26.00 |
| | 22 | Paper cups | 7.50 |
| | 29 | Cleaning supplies | 16.59 |

Check # 559 was issued.

The company follows a policy of adjusting its allowance for doubtful accounts at the end of each month. It uses the balance sheet method for estimating its doubtful accounts as follows:

| | |
|---|---|
| **Current** | **1%** |
| **Over 31-60 days** | **5%** |
| **Over 61-90 days** | **20%** |
| **Over 91+ days** | **50%** |

Print the aged detail receivable report to calculate the total expected amount that ECSS should set aside as an allowance for doubtful accounts. Remember if you do not have both Allowance for Doubtful Accounts and Bad Debt Expense account set up, you will have to add them to your chart. Record this entry in the general journal. ***Note: If the calculated total expected amount is less***

***than the balance in the Allowance for Doubtful Accounts, then NO entry is required.***

## Backing Up Data Files

Backup of data files is a very important step in the computerized accounting system. In the computerized system, when you post your transactions, the financial statements are automatically updated. To save any activity prior to posting or after posting, you can do a backup of your data files. Another use for the backup of data files would be to allow you to go back to a previous session's work, if necessary. You can copy your backup files to your working disk, and make any changes. Keep in mind that, when this is done, you will lose any work done prior to this session. The restoring of backup files will replace the existing files. When to do backups will be indicated in the practice sets.

### Making A Backup Copy

Use File Manager to make a copy of the data disk. Keep two disks to ensure backup of your data files. From the Program Manager:

- Click **Main**.
- Click **File Manager**.
- Click **Disk** from the menu.
- Click **Copy Disk**.
- Place the data disk in the disk drive as your source disk.

Follow the instructions on the screen to prompt you for the destination disk.

- Replace the source disk with destination disk.
- Click **OK**.

When the copy is made close file manager window. Label the disks appropriately.

## Printing the Financial Statements

Once all adjusting entries are recorded and posted, you should print the trial balance and the financial reports.
To print reports,

- Select **Report** from the menu bar.
- Print General Journal
  General Ledger (Optional)
  Trial Balance

Income Statement
Balance Sheet

## Analyzing Financial Statements

After entering all transactions and printing the financial statements for the month of April, write a one- page summary about the operations of the company. Include the following:

- Did the company have a net income or loss?
- How can the company increase sales and service revenue?
- Are there expenses that are in excess for the month?
- Is the inventory level appropriate for month end?
- Add any other business suggestions to the summary.

## Recording Transactions for the Month of May

During the month of May, continue with the invoice number from April.

May 1 Issued weekly payroll
Pay period: 04/24/91- 04/30/91

| | |
|---|---|
| Sarah Merritt | Salary |
| Stephen Hunter | 35.5 hours |
| Rosie Hossier | 20 hours |

1 Record bank transfer from Cash Operating to Cash Payroll.

2 Sold faucet on credit, $125.00, invoiced to Julie Homer. Inv.# 412. New customer address: 13 West Street, Leesport, PA.

3 Paid telephone bill, $75.00, to the Penn Phone Company Ck.# 560.

3 Received payments from:

| | |
|---|---|
| Zing Electricians | For Inv.# 403 Ck.# 1125 |
| Central Plumbing | $1500.00 for partial payment (principle of April 16 Note, Ck.# 221. |

4 Paid IRS withholding tax for April, Ck. # 561.

8 Issued weekly payroll for the following employees:
Pay Period: 05/01/91- 05/07/91

| | |
|---|---|
| Sarah Merritt | Salary |
| Stephen Hunter | 35 hours |
| Rosie Hossier | 30 hours |

8 Record bank transfer from Cash Operating to Cash Payroll.

11 Paid Inv.# 5777, for Uptown Hardware Supply, Ck. # 562.

12 Mr. Tom Harris, representing Nornstown Realty Associates, wants to contract for the replacement of energy-wasting hot water heaters and cracked toilets in 20 of their vacant rental units. Sarah Merritt has agreed to a flat-rate of 5 hours plumbing labor per rental unit in exchange for prepayment of labor.
New Address: 1833 Ives Street, Nornstown, PA

13 Received Ck.# 6751 for $5,000.00 from Nornstown Realty Associates as payment in advance for labor, Inv. # 413.

13 Purchased 17,500 feet of wiring from Dynamic Lighting ($0.23/ft), on credit, 3/15, n/30, Inv.# 239.

15 Paid telephone bill, Sprint, $19.75, Ck # 563.
Paid gasoline bill to Mobil Oil, $53.15, Ck.# 564.

15 Issued weekly payroll for the following employees:
Pay period: 05/08/91- 05/15/91

| | |
|---|---|
| Sarah Merritt | Salary |
| Stephen Hunter | 40 hours |
| Rosie Hossier | 25 hours |

15 Record bank transfer from Cash Operating to Cash Payroll.

15 Sold 75 circuit breakers ($7.95), 6500 feet of wiring ($0.75/ft) and 125 switches ($3.75) on credit, 2/15, n/30, to Zing Electricians, Inv# 414.

15 Purchased 30 electric water heaters ($110.00) and 30 toilets ($99.00) on credit from Hot and Cold, Inc., Inv.# 275.

16 Received payment from Taylor Samson for Inv. # 408 dated April 30, Ck.# 2142.

17 Received payment from Central Plumbing for remaining balance on April 16 note, Ck.# 1639.

18 Provided invoice for 20 electric water heaters ($225.00) and 20 toilets ($195.00) to Nornstown Realty Associates, Inv.# 415.

18 Collected interest revenue of $35.28, Ck. # 674.

19 Sold 10 electric water heaters ($225.00), 1,500 feet of wiring ($0.75 per foot), 10 circuit breakers ($7.95) and 10 switches ($3.75) on credit, 3/15 n/30, to Central Plumbing, Inv.# 416.

20 Paid state sales tax for April.

22 Issued weekly payroll:
05/16/91- 05/22/91

| | |
|---|---|
| Sarah Merritt | Salary |
| Stephen Hunter | 37.5 hours |
| Rosie Hossier | 35 hours |

22 Record bank transfer from Cash Operating to Cash Payroll.

25 Issued invoice to:
Sam Rewsbee 5,000 feet of Wire ($0.75 per foot), 24 switches ($3.75 each), Inv.# 417.

26 Received $1000.00, in advance, for plumbing labor but not yet performed for Central Plumbing, Ck. # 933.

26 Purchased 4 electric water heaters ($110.00) on credit 2/15, n/30 from Hot and Cold, Inc, Inv. # 700.

26 Issued invoice for 4 hours labor to repair a plumbing problem, Taylor Samson, Inv.# 418.

27 Returned damaged water heater to whom we made the purchase from on April 5.

27 Paid invoice dated April 5, Inv.# 210 to Hot and Cold, Inc, Ck # 565.

27 Received and paid advertising invoice for $25.00 to The Day Paper, Ck. # 566.

29 Purchased office supplies for $300.00 from City Stationery, 2/10 n/30, Inv. # 780.

29 Issued weekly payroll for the following employees:
Pay period: 05/23/91- 05/29/91

| | |
|---|---|
| Sarah Merritt | Salary |
| Stephen Hunter | 35 hours |
| Rosie Hossier | 20 hours |

29 Record bank transfer from Cash Operating to Cash Payroll.

31 Seven rental units have been completed for Nornstown Realty Associates. Adjust the appropriate accounts.

31 Recorded log book for service calls for month of May:
prepared for:

| | |
|---|---|
| Sam Rewsbee | |
| 5/5* Inv. # 419 | Replaced faucet fixtures, $125.00<br>Plumbing Labor 4 Hours |
| 5/29* Inv. # 420 | Performed wiring job using the<br>1,000 ft of wire purchased on May 15.<br>Electrical Labor 6 Hours |
| Zing Electricians | |
| 5/8* Inv. # 421 | Sold wire for swimming pool<br>500 feet wire ($0.75/ft)<br>Circuit Breaker, $7.95<br>Electrical Labor 5 Hours |
| Central Plumbing | |
| 5/26* Inv. # 422 | Heating system repaired<br>Water heater, $235.00<br>Plumbing Labor 5 hours |

*Note: Journal date 5/31

**Preparing Adjusting Entries**

Once the trial balance has been printed, make the following adjusting entries. Use ADJ as the posting reference.

May 31 Accrued interest revenue, $25.83.

May 31 Supplies on hand, $650.00

May 31 Prepaid insurance expired, $650.00

May 31 Accrued interest expense, $125.00

May 31 Depreciation expense, $200.00 for the computer; $250.00 for the automotive, $1,000 for Building.

Enter the following transaction to replenish petty cash:

| | | | |
|---|---|---|---|
| May | 15 | Coffee supplies | $22.75 |
| | 18 | Postage | 15.00 |
| | 20 | Gas for company car | 42.00 |
| | 22 | Paper cups | 7.50 |
| | 29 | Cleaning supplies | 26.59 |

Issued check # 567.

Record the Allowance from Doubtful Accounts, if necessary, using the Aged Receivable as used for the month of May.

## Recording the Transactions for the Month of June

The invoice numbers and check numbers continue from the month of May. ***Note: Supply invoice and check numbers when needed.***

June 1 Purchased 2 Kohler toilets ($99.00) on credit terms 3/15, n/30 from Waterworks and ETC. Inv.# 6524.

2 Sold electrical inventory on credit: 2 electric water heaters ($235.00 each), and 5000 feet ($0.75/ft), invoiced to AB Pipefitters, Inv.# 423 .

3 Paid phone bill, $67.75. to the Penn Phone Company, Ck.# 568.

4 Paid IRS withholding tax for May, Ck# 569.

5 Issued weekly payroll for the following employees:

Pay period: 05/30/91 - 06/04/91.

| | |
|---|---|
| Sarah Merritt | Salary |
| Stephen Hunter | 34 hours |
| Rosie Hossier | 36 hours |

5 Record bank transfer from Cash Operating to Cash Payroll.

7 Merchandise return for one toilet to Waterworks and ETC, invoice dated June 1.

12 Issued weekly payroll for the following employees:
Pay period: 06/05/91 - 06/11/91

| | |
|---|---|
| Sarah Merritt | Salary |
| Stephen Hunter | 35 hours |
| Rosie Hossier | 25 hours |

12 Record bank transfer from Cash Operating to Cash Payroll.

15 Paid telephone bill, Sprint, $41.50, Ck.# 570.
Paid gasoline bill to Mobil Oil, $72.50, Ck.# 571.

16 Paid invoice dated June 1, Ck. # 572.

17 The installation labor for the thirteen remaining rental units of Nornstown Realty Associates have been completed. Adjust the appropriate accounts.

18 Collected interest revenue of $25.83, Ck # 435.

18 Sent invoice for additional materials at the rental unit installations to Nornstown Realty Associates: 9 circuit breakers ($7.95) and 300 feet of wiring ($0.75/ft), Inv.# 424.

19 Paid state sales tax for May, Ck# 573.

19 Issued weekly payroll for the following employees:
Pay period: 06/12/91 - 06/19/91

| | |
|---|---|
| Sarah Merritt | Salary |
| Stephen Hunter | 40 hours |
| Rosie Hossier | 20 hours |

19 Record bank transfer from Cash Operating to Cash Payroll.

22 Received payment of balance from AB Pipefitters, Ck # 487.

26 Repaired plumbing, 4 labor hours on credit to Sam Rewsbee Inv.# 425 .

26 Issued invoice for 3 hours electrical labor to repair a faulty wire, Zing Electricians, Inv.# 426.

26 Issued weekly payroll for the following employees:
Pay Period: 06/20/91- 06/26/91

| | |
|---|---|
| Sarah Merritt | Salary |
| Stephen Hunter | 40 hours |
| Rosie Hossier | 25 hours |

26 Record bank transfer from Cash Operating to Cash Payroll.

27 Received and paid advertising invoice for $30.00 to The Day Paper, Ck# 574 .

29 Purchased store supplies for $350.00 from City Stationery, 2/10 n/30, Inv.# 613.

30 Received payment from Zing Electricians for Inv# 350 and Inv# 415.

30 Recorded Log Book for Service calls for the month of June:
Invoices prepared for:

| | |
|---|---|
| J.R. Sering (new customer) | |
| 6/5* Inv. # 427 | Replaced faucet fixtures<br>Faucet, $130.00<br>Plumbing Labor 2 Hours |
| AB Pipefitters | |
| 6/9* Inv. # 428 | Wired inground swimming pool<br>5200 feet wire ($0.75 per foot)<br>Circuit Breaker, $7.95<br>Electrical Labor 3 Hours |
| Nornstown Realty | |
| 6/23* Inv. # 429 | Replaced leaky faucets<br>7 faucets ($129.00)<br>Plumbing Labor 6 hours |
| Taylor Sampson<br>6/25* Inv. # 430 | Rental cottage repairs to sink<br>Sink, $190.00<br>Plumbing Labor 2 hours |

*Note: Journal Date 6/30

**Preparing Adjusting Entries**

Once the trial balance has been printed, make the following adjusting entries. Use ADJ as the posting reference.

| | | |
|---|---|---|
| June | 30 | Accrued interest revenue, $27.50. |
| June | 30 | Supplies on hand, $250.00 |
| June | 30 | Prepaid insurance expired, $650.00 |
| June | 30 | Depreciation expense, $200.00 for the computer, $1,000 for building and $250 for automobile. |
| June | 30 | Balance of Unearned plumbing revenue, $450.00 |

Enter the following transaction to replenish petty cash:

| | | | |
|---|---|---|---|
| June | 15 | Coffee supplies | $22.75 |
| | 20 | Gas for company car | 33.50 |
| | 22 | Paper cups | 7.50 |
| | 29 | Cleaning supplies | 16.59 |

Issued check # 575.

Record the Allowance from Doubtful Accounts using the Aged Receivable as used for the month of April.

## Backing Up Data Files

Backup of data files is a very important step in the computerized accounting system. In the computerized system, when you post your transactions, the financial statements are automatically updated. To save any activity prior to posting or after posting, you can do a backup of your data files. Another use for the backup of data files would be to allow you to go back to a previous session's work, if necessary. You can copy your backup files to your working disk, and make any changes. Keep in mind that, when this is done, you will lose any work done prior to this session. The restoring of backup files will replace the existing files. When to do backups will be indicated in the practice sets.

### Making A Backup Copy

Use File Manager to make a copy of the data disk. Keep two disks to ensure backup of your data files. From the Program Manager:

- Click **Main**.
- Click **File Manager**.

- Click **Disk** from the menu.
- Click **Copy Disk**.
- Place the data disk in the disk drive as your source disk.

Follow the instructions on the screen to prompt you for the destination disk.

- Replace the source disk with destination disk.
- Click **OK**.

When the copy is made close file manager window. Label the disks appropriately.

## Printing the Financial Statements

Once all adjusting entries are recorded and posted, you should print the trial balance and the financial reports.
To print reports,
Select **Reports** from the menu bar.

- Print General Journal
  General Ledger
  Trial Balance
  Income Statement
  Balance Sheet
  Payroll Reports

## Exiting CA-Simply

After completing the transactions and printing all reports, you should and exit CA-Simply.
**To Exit CA-Simply:**
Click the **Control** menu bar in the upper left corner OR
Click **File**, then Click **Exit**.

## Chapter Summary

You have computerized the last three months of transaction for ECSS, Inc. You can now computerize any company and use the appropriate modules to ensure the efficient and accurate operation of a business.

# APPENDIX A

## Sample Financial Statements for Energy Connection, Inc.

**The Energy Connection**
**Balance Sheet** As At 4/1/91

| | | |
|---|---|---|
| ASSETS | | |
| **Current Assets** | | |
| Cash -Operating | | 38,874.73 |
| Cash-Payroll | | 0.00 |
| Petty Cash | | 100.00 |
| Accounts Receivable | 12,501.35 | |
| Allowance for Doubtful Accts | -500.00 | |
| Net Realizable Value | | 12,001.35 |
| Notes Receivable- Short Term | | 3,000.00 |
| Inventory -Electrical | | 4,620.00 |
| Inventory-Plumbing | | 4,950.00 |
| Office Supplies | | 852.00 |
| Prepaid Insurance | | 2,400.00 |
| **Total Current Assets** | | 66,798.08 |
| **Plant Assets** | | |
| Land | | 60,000.00 |
| Buildings | 150,000.00 | |
| Accum Depr-Building | -30,000.00 | |
| Subtotal | | 120,000.00 |
| Automotives | 65,000.00 | |
| Accum Depr-Automotives | -12,000.00 | |
| Subtotal | | 53,000.00 |
| Computers | 5,200.00 | |
| Accum Depr-Computers | -800.00 | |
| Subtotal | | 4,400.00 |
| **Total Plant Assets** | | 237,400.00 |
| TOTAL ASSETS | | 304,198.08 |
| LIABILITIES | | |
| **Current Liabilities** | | |
| Accounts Payable | | 5,147.00 |
| Notes Payable -Short Term | | 12,000.00 |
| FIT Tax Payable | | 428.95 |
| FICA Payable | | 554.65 |
| FUTA Payable | | 82.25 |
| SIT Payable | | 770.35 |
| SUTA Payable | | 24.90 |
| Pension Plan Payable | | 5,200.00 |
| Employee Insurance Payable | | 0.00 |
| Sales Tax Payable | | 1,725.35 |
| Medicar Tax Payable | | 0.00 |
| Unearned Electrical Revenue | | 275.00 |
| Unearned Plumbling Revenue | | 200.00 |
| **Total Current Liabilities** | | 26,408.45 |
| **Long Term Liabilities** | | |
| Note Payable-Sarah Merritt | | 52,000.00 |
| **Total Long Term Liabilities** | | 52,000.00 |
| TOTAL LIABILITIES | | 78,408.45 |
| EQUITY | | |
| **Stockholders' Equity** | | |
| Common Stock | | 30,000.00 |
| Retained Earnings | | 195,789.63 |
| Current Earnings | | 0.00 |
| **Total Stockholders' Equity** | | 225,789.63 |
| TOTAL EQUITY | | 225,789.63 |
| LIABILITIES AND EQUITY | | 304,198.08 |

**The Energy Connection**
**Income Statement** 4/1/91 to 4/1/91

| | |
|---|---|
| **REVENUE** | |
| **Sales Revenue** | |
| Sales Electrical | 0.00 |
| Sales -Plumbing | 0.00 |
| **Total Net Sales** | 0.00 |
| **Service Revenue** | |
| Service -Electrical | 0.00 |
| Service -Plumbing | 0.00 |
| **Total Service Revenue** | 0.00 |
| **Other Revenue and Expenses** | |
| Interest Revenue | 0.00 |
| Sales and Service Discounts | 0.00 |
| **Total Other Revenue and Expenses** | 0.00 |
| **TOTAL REVENUE** | 0.00 |
| **EXPENSE** | |
| **Cost of Goods Sold** | |
| Cost of Goods Sold -Electrical | 0.00 |
| Cost of Goods Sold -Plumbing | 0.00 |
| **Total Cost of Goods Sold** | 0.00 |
| **Operating Expenses** | |
| Wages Expense | 0.00 |
| Medicare Tax Expense | 0.00 |
| FICA Tax Expense | 0.00 |
| FUTA Tax Expense | 0.00 |
| SUTA Tax Expense | 0.00 |
| Fuel Expense | 0.00 |
| Insurance Expense | 0.00 |
| Repair Expense | 0.00 |
| Office Supplies Expense | 0.00 |
| Telephone Expense | 0.00 |
| Utilities Expense | 0.00 |
| Advertising Expense | 0.00 |
| License Expense | 0.00 |
| Depreciation Expense | 0.00 |
| Rent Expense | 0.00 |
| Interest Expense | 0.00 |
| Bank Charges | 0.00 |
| **Total Operating Expenses** | 0.00 |
| **TOTAL EXPENSE** | 0.00 |
| **NET INCOME** | 0.00 |